Recommendation
An Interac...

There are few crises that can face a human that are not greatly diminished by a robust sense of gratitude. It may be the strongest predictor of satisfaction in life. Wayne convincingly presents the importance, potential, and barriers to gratitude, as well as scriptural mentors and practical skill sets for cultivating that "attitude of gratitude."

—**Dr. Chris Legg,** therapist

In the sometimes angry and bitter world we find ourselves in, it is time for Christians to say a good word about gratitude. In this delightful book, Wayne Braudrick offers a biblical response and a call to thankfulness. *The Power of a Merry Heart* is a message we all need to hear.

—**George M. Hillman Jr., PhD,**
Vice President of Student Life, Dean of Students
Dallas Theological Seminary

Complaining seems to be the default mode of conversation these days. Despite enjoying a higher standard of living, more leisure time, and better medical care than virtually any other society in history, griping about trivialities can usually find common ground with most people, and I'm as guilty as anyone. Here, Dr. Braudrick shows from Scripture how sinful and silly this attitude is. He also provides the tools and admonition to help us overcome such ingratitude. Appropriately so, I'm very thankful for this book.

—**Dr. Mark Huffman,** physician & author

About the same time that I received an early draft of this book, I heard a secular "healthy living" presentation that attempted to teach a shallower version of *The Power of a Merry Heart*. While the world may only now be waking up to this reality, it's hardly new. Proverbs 17:22 tells us "a merry heart does good, like medicine." In this work, Dr Braudrick reveals the impact of gratitude on both our physical and mental health, and its consequences in both the temporal and eternal realms. This is a timely reminder for us all.

—**Paul Hahn,** inventor

I deeply appreciate Dr. Braudrick's work in *The Power of a Merry Heart* because he reminds Christians that gratitude and thanksgiving teach us that we are, in fact, dependent people who enjoy the unmerited grace of God. Through a combination of his always-pastoral tone, practical suggestions, and well-researched material, Wayne's book gives each of us the opportunity to cultivate one of the most fundamental and influential parts of our Christian character. You will find this devotional a helpful resource as you seek to turn away from selfishness, bitterness, and pride in your own life. It will remind you of the truth of the Gospel in a way that will encourage you to express your gratitude not just in words, but also in service – both towards God and other people. I commend it to you!

—**Matt Lantz,** pastor

ALL THE DIFFERENCE SERIES

The Power of a Merry Heart

For Such a Time as This

Whatever Happened to Manhood?

Whatever Happened to Manhood? Study Guide

Luke's Curious Christmas

Forthcoming:

Your Work Matters

In the Name of Love

To Nineveh—Going Overboard for a Lost Generation

WAYNE BRAUDRICK

THE POWER OF A *Merry* HEART

An Interactive Workbook on GRATITUDE

The Power of a Merry Heart:
An Interactive Workbook on Gratitude
Copyright © 2017 Wayne Braudrick
All rights reserved.

No part of this book may be reproduced in any form or by any electronic or mechanical means including information storage and retrieval systems, without permission in writing from the author. The only exception is by a reviewer, who may quote short excerpts in a review.

Lampion Press, LLC
P. O. Box 932
Silverton, OR 97381

Scripture quotations marked (NASB) are taken from the New American Standard Bible, Copyright 1960, 1962, 1963, 1968, 1972, 1973, 1975, 1977, 1995 by the Lockman Foundation. Used by permission. (www.Lockman.org)

Scripture quotations marked (NKJV) are taken from the New King James Version®. Copyright © 1982 by Thomas Nelson. Used by permission. All rights reserved.

"Scripture quotations marked (ESV) are from The Holy Bible, English Standard Version® (ESV®), copyright © 2001 by Crossway, a publishing ministry of Good News Publishers. Used by permission. All rights reserved."

Scripture quotations marked (HCSB) are taken from the Holman Christian Standard Bible®, Copyright © 1999, 2000, 2002, 2003, 2009 by Holman Bible Publishers. Used by permission. Holman Christian Standard Bible®, Holman CSB®, and HCSB® are federally registered trademarks of Holman Bible Publishers.

Scripture quotations marked (NLT) are taken from the Holy Bible, New Living Translation, copyright © 1996, 2004, 2007 by Tyndale House Foundation. Used by permission of Tyndale House Publishers, Inc., Carol Stream, IL 60188. All rights reserved.

Scripture quotations marked (TLB) are taken from The Living Bible copyright © 1971. Used by permission of Tyndale House Publishers, Inc., Carol Stream, Illinois 60188. All rights reserved.

Scripture quoted by permission. Quotations designated (NET) are from the NET Bible® copyright ©1996-2006 by Biblical Studies Press, L.L.C. http://netbible.com All rights reserved.

The names: THE NET BIBLE®, NEW ENGLISH TRANSLATION COPYRIGHT (c) 1996 BY BIBLICAL STUDIES PRESS, L.L.C. NET Bible® IS A REGISTERED TRADEMARK THE NET BIBLE® LOGO, SERVICE MARK COPYRIGHT (c) 1997 BY BIBLICAL STUDIES PRESS, L.L.C. ALL RIGHTS RESERVED

ISBN: 978-1-942614-32-6

Formatting and cover design by Amy Cole, JPL Design Solutions

Printed in the United States of America

DEDICATION

To Judy and Kent Marshall,
world record writers of thank you notes

CONTENTS

Introduction 1

CHAPTER 1: Gratitude Changes Everything 5

CHAPTER 2: Overcoming the Enemies of Thankfulness 21

CHAPTER 3: Live with a Genuine Attitude of Gratitude 39

CHAPTER 4: Fostering Gratitude 55

Acknowledgements 75

Endnotes 77

About the Author 81

INTRODUCTION

This little book has a very simple and important goal: that you and I enjoy an attitude of gratitude and encourage the same in others. There are very few things as life-transformative as gratitude, and yet it appears to be one of the least-utilized biblical practices. From the beginning, God has known and shown that a merry heart benefits the human immensely. That why His thanksgiving commands in Moses' Law contain this insight: "When you sacrifice a thanksgiving offering to the Lord, you must sacrifice it so that it is acceptable for *your* benefit." (Leviticus 22:29 NET, emphasis added)

Notice the Lord's desire that the person benefits from thanksgiving. YHWH's plan is that people are blessed by the amazing changes that come into the life of one who is thankful. John Milton, writing during a tumultuous era when it was surely difficult for biblical Christians to feel gratitude, summarized the power of thanksgiving this way:

> A grateful mind
> By owing owes not, but still pays, at once
> Indebted and discharg'd.[1]

By sinful nature, we humans are ungrateful. We are marked by bitterness, grudges, fears, covetousness, entitlement, and isolation. As Mark Twain noted, "If you pick up a starving dog and make him prosperous, he will not bite you. This is the principal difference between a dog and a man."[2]

Holy God, desiring for us to enjoy a redeemed relationship with Him and with our brethren, established the practice of giving thanks. When we practice gratitude, we are drawn closer to God and made more winsome toward people. The Apostle Paul captures the import of thanksgiving as we live out these relationships, writing: "Therefore, as you have received Christ Jesus the Lord, so walk in Him, having been firmly rooted and now being built up in Him and established in your faith, just as you were instructed, and overflowing with gratitude." (Colossians 2:6-7 NASB) Business consultant David Horsager explains what "overflowing with gratitude" achieves among human relationships, saying: "Gratitude is the number one factor in being attractive to people and building trust with them."[3]

Of course, the reality is that we all endure much about which we understandably feel ungrateful. This is a broken world. Despite our justification in Christ, the Christian still battles his flesh while our enemy works diligently to demonize our lives. Thus, we find ourselves regularly wounded and wounding. As James summarizes: "For in many things we offend all." (James 3:2 KJV) Gratitude often seems absurd or at best it appears very difficult. This study is designed to change that natural reaction. God has made thanksgiving a critical part of His perfect plan for His redeemed community. Understanding that and learning to practice gratitude has positive repercussions that are almost impossible to overstate. That's why Paul's bottom line on gratitude is unequivocal. Note the ubiquitous aspect of thanksgiving in these passages:

> In *everything* give thanks; for this is God's will for you in Christ Jesus. (1 Thessalonians 5:18 NASB, emphasis added)
>
> And do not get drunk with wine, for that is debauchery, but be filled with the Spirit, addressing one another in psalms and hymns and spiritual songs, singing and making melody to the Lord with your heart, giving thanks *always and for everything* to God the Father in the name of our Lord Jesus Christ, submitting to one another out of reverence for Christ. (Ephesians 5:18-21 ESV, emphasis added)

You and I have many legitimate pains this side of heaven, and it is scripturally right and good that we cry out to the Lord about those hurts and fears. Nonetheless, we can and must learn to be thankful as well. A pastor I know nailed the biblical ideal when I called and asked him how he was doing after an incredibly stormy season in which his church had fired him. He said: "Contentment has nothing to do with what's in my hand. It has everything to do with what's in my heart."

CHAPTER 1

GRATITUDE CHANGES EVERYTHING

> **THEME:** We examine why thanksgiving is important, what gratitude is, and what it changes in our lives.
>
> **OBJECTIVE:** That we give thanks with grateful hearts.

Todd Sinelli is a friend of mine. He's a wise young man, a talented teacher, and a pretty fine magician. Once when we were teaching at a conference together, Todd and I got to talking about a little side point that really captivated each of us. We found ourselves discussing gratitude. There were many other important issues that came up—life, churches, growth in Jesus—but everything always seemed to work its way back to the topic of thankfulness.

Not wanting the conversation to end, we later arranged to meet in a town halfway between our respective cities. There, over dinner shared with our sweethearts, Sinelli, the girls, and I continued investigating the need for gratitude. Looking at the world, the state of churches today, and our own souls, we concluded that a reminder is called for. Folks today need to live by the scriptural truth that God wants His people to regularly experience gratitude. That was the takeaway from our dialogues, and it's the big idea that led to this book.

GOD WANTS HIS PEOPLE TO REGULARLY EXPERIENCE GRATITUDE.

That's why He establishes the thanksgiving offering. In the Old Testament Law, God establishes a very important series of regulatory reminders that are collectively referred to as "the thanksgiving offering." Leviticus 22 has an exemplary statement: "When you sacrifice a thanksgiving offering to the Lord, you must sacrifice it so that it is acceptable for your benefit. On that very day it must be eaten; you must not leave any part of it over until morning. I am the Lord." (Leviticus 22:29-30 NET)

The original Hebrew is pretty cool. Two of the key words are transliterated *zebah todah*. *Zebah* [zay' vah] is a multifaceted term for sacrifice. It means an offering to God, but it carries two other important connotations:

#1—It means bright, joyful, and dedicated to God. That's likely why it came into modern Hebrew as Ziva—a girl's name. By the way, I always thought they would kill off the character Ziva David on the television show NCIS. Because her name in ancient Hebrew meant "joyful sacrifice of David," I figured the producers would have her die offering her life for others.

#2—*Zebah* also means a meal. That's special connotation #2. A *zebah* sacrifice was an offering that was especially joyful because God expected it to be eaten as a feast. In fact, Leviticus 22:30 makes it clear that the Lord expects the whole feast to be consumed in one big sitting. This wasn't gluttony (although the food police of our day would likely deem it so.) God wanted His people to regularly have a big blowout meal with Him.

And what was this big meal to be all about? Giving thanks! Our second important Hebrew word is *todah* [toe dah']. It's a special word that means gratitude that changes a person. You see, *todah* means thank you…but it's more. There is a depth to this term. Inside and outside of the Bible we see *todah* used as a word for confession. *Todah* means that one is grateful to God, and that expression of gratitude causes one to think differently.

When a person feasts regularly with God in gratitude, that person confesses that God is incredibly good. She is reminded of how this expression of thanksgiving should be continuous. He begins to understand just how ungrateful most of his life really is. Zebah-todah is a life-changing practice.

And that's why God *commanded* it for His followers. He knows that those who need *zebah-todah* the most are the least likely to practice it on their own initiative. In a *Wall Street Journal* article, Diana Kapp summarized this way:

> Gratitude works like a muscle. Take time to recognize good fortune, and feelings of appreciation can increase. Even more, those who are less grateful gain the most from a concerted effort. "Gratitude treatments are most effective in those least grateful," says Eastern Washington University psychology professor Philip Watkins.[4]

Zebah-todah is life changing. Just consider this experiment: 122 elementary school children were taught a weeklong curriculum about gratitude and giving. The study, published in *School Psychology Review*, showed that gratefulness and other positive traits grew considerably as teachers focused the students on gratitude. And the heightened thankfulness translated into action. Amazingly, 44% of the kids in the gratitude curriculum opted to write thank-you notes when given the choice following a PTA presentation. In the control group, only 25% wrote notes. That was after a PTA meeting! I have sat through many many dozens of those important yet routinely boring meeting and never even considered writing a thank you. (For which I am now chagrined. Thanks, kids!)

Ms. Kapp shares these great insights:

> "The old adage that virtues are caught, not taught, applies here," says University of California, Davis psychology professor Robert Emmons. Parents need to model this behavior to build their children's gratitude muscle. "It's not what parents want to hear, but you cannot give your kids something that you yourselves do not have," Dr. Emmons says. This may seem obvious, but it eludes many parents, [according to] Dr. Watkins. "I think the most important thing for us adults to realize is we're not very grateful either," he says.[5]

God knew His people are by nature ungrateful. That's why He focused part of His curriculum on zebah-todah. "But," you are asking in your bored voice reserved for PTA meetings, "Wasn't that just for Hebrew peoples in the old covenant?" I'm so glad you asked. The answer is "No. Not hardly."

God carries the principle into the New Covenant. For example, think through the command in the Colossians' letter of the New Testament: "Therefore, as you received Christ Jesus the Lord, so walk in him, rooted and built up in him and established in the faith, just as you were taught, abounding in thanksgiving." (Colossians 2:6-7 ESV)

In the Old Testament, God makes it clear that people are developed when they appreciate all the remarkable, miraculous blessings of life like rain, breathing, food, love. Then, in the New Testament, thanksgiving is expanded to especially include gratitude for the spiritual redemption found in the great gift of Jesus. And the Apostle Paul is very vocal about this. Through him, God commands believers in Jesus:

To give thanks in all things	Rom 14:6; 1 Thes 5:18
To give thanks as Jesus did; in His name	1 Cor 11:24; Eph 5:20
To make thanks part of prayer requests	Phil 4:6
To abound in thanksgiving	Col 2:7
To be alert for thanksgiving opportunities	Col 4:2

This is God's New Testament curriculum—to give thanks in Christ. Years ago, Christian writers Ed Nalle and Mark Altrogge tried to summarize all this New Testament gratitude in a poem. His band Glad recorded it and the song became a hit on the Christian charts:

You did not wait for me
to draw near to You
But You clothed Yourself
with frail humanity
You did not wait for me
to cry out to You
But You let me hear Your voice
calling me
And I'm forever grateful to You

> I'm forever grateful for the cross
> I'm forever grateful to You
> That You came to seek and save the lost.
> —Mark Altrogge, "Forever Grateful"[6]

I think Paul would applaud that take on Colossians 2. Later, a songwriter who grew up near my home tried to capture both the Old and New Testament lessons on gratitude. Billy Crockett wrote a beautiful song called "Thankful Boys and Girls" which had these lyrics:

> Let us be thankful boys and girls
> For eyes and ears and toes
> And puppies with wet noses

> Let us be thankful boys and girls
> For lessons we have learned
> And love we have not earned

> Let us be thankful boys and girls
> —Billy Crockett, "Thankful Boys and Girls"[7]

IS DISCIPLINED PRACTICE NEEDED?

Those thoughts about thankfulness are beautiful! But, is such practice really necessary? Is there really a need to tell people, remind people, and teach people to be grateful? Doesn't gratitude just come naturally? Some thinkers, including the French Renaissance writer, monk, and humanist Rabelais (1494-1593) and the English lawyer and stateman Sir Thomas More (1478-1535), assumed thankfulness will flow instinctively.

In case you've never bumped into them, each of those guys wrote very famous eutopian books—stories describing the ideal society. They decided that such a society could exist because humans are basically good and grateful. At least that's what Rabelais thought. More may have been cagier—after all, he dropped the E from the title of his book *Utopia*. That changed his book title from Eu-topia meaning "good place" to U-topia, meaning "no place."

Regardless of titles, these dudes fired up a tune as old as Plato and as current as most speeches given in today's U.S. Senate—declaring that humans are basically good and will be happy, holy, and grateful all on their own. Samuel Clemens, who wrote under the name Mark Twain, disagreed heartily. Remember the quote we referenced in the introduction from Twain's sarcastic classic *Pudd'nhead Wilson:* "If you pick up a starving dog and make him prosperous, he will not bite you. This is the principal difference between a dog and a man."

Mr. Twain/Clemens is correct. The Bible is very clear on this—the norm for humanity is to be very ungrateful. As just one scripture among hundreds on this topic, let's look at Galatians 5: "Now the deeds of the flesh are evident, which are: immorality, impurity, sensuality, idolatry, sorcery, enmities, strife, jealousy, outbursts of anger, disputes, dissensions, factions, envying, drunkenness, carousing, and things like these, of which I forewarn you, just as I have forewarned you, that those who practice such things will not inherit the kingdom of God. (Galatians 5:19-21 NASB)

That is the base setting of humanity: separated from God and the opposite of grateful. Yes, the image of God still exists in fallen people. God's blueprint has not been erased…but the imprint has been defaced. This is why God empowers Christians through His Spirit to be thankful boys and girls. This is why He repeats His commands for us to show appreciation—because at our core we are stinkers who bite the hand that feeds us.

As I thought all this through in preparation for this volume, I came up with the following premise or reason why we should study the topic:

> By sinful nature, we humans are ungrateful. We are marked by bitterness, grudges, fears, covetousness, entitlement, and isolation. Holy God, desiring to enjoy a redeemed relationship with us, established the practice of giving thanks. When we practice gratitude, we are drawn closer to God and made more winsome toward people.

Of course, I know what most of us are thinking after reading that premise. We're thinking that only applies to *other* people. We are smugly looking at our neighbor, considering how that statement is so true of them, and saying to ourselves, "Well, thank goodness I'm not like that!"

Or are we? Let me give you a little quiz I have put together, based on the fine work of some research psychologists. Grab a pen or pencil and in your book please answer this brief gratitude quiz.[8] Just put a mark beside the answer that most honestly describes you.

A. It is important to appreciate things such as health, family, and friends.

1. __ I strongly disagree.
2. __ I somewhat disagree.
3. __ I somewhat agree.
4. __ I wholeheartedly agree.

B. I am most likely to notice and/or comment on:

1. __ the painful or unhealthy aspects of my life
2. __ painful things more often than joyful ones
3. __ joyful things more often than painful ones
4. __ the joyful or healthy aspects of my life

C. I feel very thankful for my degree of physical health.

1. __ Never
2. __ Once a year
3. __ Once in a while
4. __ Regularly

D. I thank God for what He provides.

1. __ Never
2. __ Once a year
3. __ Once in a while
4. __ Regularly

E. Though I may not have everything I want, I am thankful for what I have.

1. __ I strongly disagree.
2. __ I somewhat disagree.
3. __ I somewhat agree.
4. __ I wholeheartedly agree.

F. I reflect on the worst times in my life to help me realize both how they were used to develop me and how fortunate I am now.

1. __ Never
2. __ Once a year
3. __ Once in a while
4. __ Regularly

G. I remind myself how fortunate I am to have the privileges and opportunities I have encountered in life.

1. __ Never
2. __ Once a year
3. __ Once in a while
4. __ Regularly

H. I demand more or better things.

1. __ Regularly
2. __ Once in a while
3. __ Once a year
4. __ Never

I. I complain or point out flaws.

1. __ Regularly
2. __ Only if something really bugs me
3. __ Never
4. __ Only to build others up

J. I really notice and acknowledge the good things I receive.

1. __ Never
2. __ Once a year
3. __ Once in a while
4. __ Regularly

K. My day is ruined when my team or political candidate loses.

1. __ Every time
2. __ Usually
3. __ Sometimes
4. __ Never

L. I should build regular habits that remind me to be grateful.

1. __ I strongly disagree.
2. __ I somewhat disagree.
3. __ I somewhat agree.
4. __ I wholeheartedly agree.

OK, let's see how necessary this all really is. Let's go through our scoring:

1. Add the numbers of all the responses you enumerated. Each #1 = 1 point, #2 = 2 points, #3 = 3 points, #4 = 4 points.

2. Got it? Now, subtract 4 points because you did your own scoring. The research is very clear that people score themselves at least 30% more positively than objective others would. Therefore, if you want a real read, subtract 4 points. Stop whining; all you're doing is proving how ungrateful you are!

3. Now, here's the breakdown:

- If you scored 37-48, you have a high gratitude score. Praise God! Keep developing your attitude of gratitude.

- If you were in the 25-36 range, you have an above median gratitude score. That's good, but you are almost certainly missing out on many of the benefits of responding to God's call for thanksgiving as part of your regular routine.

- If your adjusted total was 13-24, you have a below average gratitude score. Scripture calls for you to let the Spirit of God develop better gratitude practices in your life. Dr. Robert Emmons' research suggests that "A strong tendency to practice gratitude brings you more positive emotions, better health, stronger relationships, and greater life satisfaction."[9]

- And if you ranked from 0-12, I don't really know what to say. You really can't score this low without trying very diligently. So, I would say, "Be grateful for your capacity to show such diligent commitment;" but you wouldn't. Seriously, I implore you to consider the blockades to gratitude in your life.

WHAT GRATITUDE ACCOMPLISHES.

We all display the biblical truth that by nature we don't fulfill God's command to practice gratitude always. But, that begs another question—what does gratitude accomplish? Suppose I get with God's appreciation program. What will that change?

It's a good question and scripture offers great answers. First, gratitude changes one's experiential relationship with God. Look again at the Leviticus 22 command: "When you sacrifice a thanksgiving offering to the LORD, you must sacrifice it so that it is acceptable for your benefit. On that very day it must be eaten; you must not leave any part of it over until morning. I am the LORD." (Leviticus 22:29-30 NET)

Notice the phrase "acceptable for your benefit." The Hebrew word *ratson*. [rat sone'] is a fascinating word. It often means "accepted." Other times *ratson* means "delight or benefit," and occasionally it's all the above—accepted and beneficial. The experts I trust most tell me that in this context the most likely meaning is both. The thanksgiving offering was not just to be done in a way that honored God and was acceptable to Him. It was meant to be enjoyed as a delightful benefit for the human worshipper as well.

Just consider for a moment how you feel when you give thanks. When you are grateful for something or someone, what does that accomplish for you? Scribble a few words in the space below. When I express gratitude, it does this for me:

However you expressed it, the response is universally positive. Studies have proven that thanksgiving lowers blood pressure and releases endorphins (hormones that convey happiness in the brain). And Scripture declares that gratitude builds up your soul in relation to the Great Provider. *Ratson*! When you and I give thanks to God, it changes us and helps develop our healthy relationship with Him. That's why the *New International Dictionary of Old Testament Theology and Exegesis* declares: "The goal of [the Thanksgiving offering] was to maintain a proper relationship between the LORD (who dwelt in the tabernacle) and Israelites in whose midst the tabernacle was pitched."[10] Gratefulness changes one's relating with God. It also changes one's inner contentment. Proverbs 23:7 states that as a person thinks inside, so is that person. Specifically, the context is describing a wretchedly selfish, ungrateful person. And as we've seen, that is our base setting. But by God's grace through Jesus, things don't have to stay that way! Consider Ephesians 5:

> And do not get drunk with wine, for that is dissipation, but be filled with the Spirit, speaking to one another in psalms and hymns and spiritual songs, singing and making melody with your heart to the Lord; always giving thanks for all things in the name of our Lord Jesus Christ to God, even the Father (Ephesians 5:18-20 NASB)

Notice that Paul is addressing internal issues here. When you let alcohol or other narcotics control you internally, that is dissipation. It's wasteful. It achieves nothing good. Let the Spirit control you instead, and you will overflow with internal joy and gratitude. This world is full of fools who think some substance will make them happy. In reality, only a thankful heart can do so.

Phil Vischer obviously had this truth in mind when he wrote this great song for his Veggie Tales videos:

> I thank God for this day,
> For the sun in the sky,
> For my mom and my dad,
> For my piece of apple pie!
> For our home on the ground,
> For His love that's all around,
> That's why I say thanks every day!
> Because a thankful heart is a happy heart!
> I'm glad for what I have,
> That's an easy way to start!
> For the love that He shares,
> 'Cause He listens to my prayers,
> That's why I say thanks every day![11]

Gratitude changes one's inner sense of contentment. My friend Todd Sinelli wrote a nifty little book called *True Riches* in which he shared these insights:

> Now, the best answer I have ever heard to the question "What does it mean to be rich?" is by Sir John Marks Templeton. Templeton is a multibillionaire and the founder of Templeton Mutual Funds. He has spent a great part of his life handling and investing large sums of money. When asked about his definition of being rich, he said it could be summed up in just one word—gratitude. He explained that if a person has five dollars to his name and is thankful for that five dollars, he is richer than the person who has five *million* dollars and wants five million more.

> To Templeton, gratitude is what makes a person rich. In his book *Discovering the Laws of Life,* Templeton writes that we should develop a spirit of thanksgiving. Each moment holds something for which we can be thankful. We can be thankful for so many simple things—like good health or a sunny day. We can be glad that we are alive and able to breathe clean air and wear dry clothes. When we start thinking of things to be thankful for our lists can grow and grow: friends, teachers, pastors, schools, libraries, dogs, and cats. Templeton may be right. Being rich can be defined in one word—*gratitude.*[12]

Amen? Indeed. Now, I was discussing all this with Paul Hahn, one of our church Elders, and he had an interesting observation on the lack of inner contentment in so many Christians. He said:

I've always found fellow believers who were waiting for some future event for satisfaction—a mindset that can prevent us seeing God's goodness today! And this phenomenon transcends age groups. Consider:

- the 11-year-old girl who can't wait until she's 13 and is finally "all grown up"
- the 14-year-old boy who can't wait until he's 16 and can drive
- the 21-year-old who thinks life will begin when he graduates college
- those desperate to be married or have children to "complete" their lives[13]

Isn't that true! And Paul went on to describe people waiting for job promotions, for the kids to move out, to finally retire, and any other number of things that tantalize with the lie of future happiness. Meanwhile God grants His grace and presence and love *now*! Those who learn to appreciate His great blessings in the now gain life-changing contentment.

That's what gratitude accomplishes. And it achieves one more thing—thankfulness changes one's relations with others. Look at these words from Leviticus 7: "And the flesh of the sacrifice of his peace offerings for thanksgiving shall be eaten on the day of his offering. He shall not leave any of it until the morning." (Leviticus 7:15 ESV)

You might say, "OK...um...why does that matter?" Think it through, friend. This is talking about a whole animal—a large animal carved, roasted, and served for a special thanksgiving meal. This isn't just *one* steak; this isn't even describing a side of beef; it's two sides and two forequarters as well. It's a lot of food!

The only way to have none left is to eat it all that day. And the only way to do that is to throw a party. When your neighbor fulfills his thanksgiving offering, you get to enjoy a courtyard barbeque together (they didn't really have backyards, but they did sit around the courtyard). God set this offering up so that it would force people to eat and celebrate together—a practice that touches something significant in human relations. Remember businessman David Horsager's note in our book introduction? "Gratitude is the number one factor in being attractive to people and building trust with them."[14]

In other words, business leaders are catching up to what God put in place 3500 years ago. We are learning the ancient truth that gratitude builds up one's relationships and even draws us into new friendships. Thankfulness changes everything—with self, God, and others. *All The Difference* (the radio ministry where I teach), received a letter that illustrates this perfectly:

> Dear Dr. B—The other day my husband had brain surgery. As you know, the waiting is intense. After a few hours, we were very relieved to meet with the doctor and hear that all had gone perfectly. He told us the good news and instructed us to go to a different waiting room while my man was brought through recovery. We walked in to the waiting room with hearts full of gratitude.
>
> In the room, there was a younger gentleman sitting in the corner talking on the phone. We overheard him say something about someone passing and that he charged up his

credit card to fly down here. He was asking them if they knew of a church or anyone that could help him because he was $40 short for a hotel room. He then made another call to share his sad news and told that person that his parents were in Ukraine on a mission trip and were flying in tomorrow.

My son and I looked at each other and knew we had to give him the money. About that time, the hospital called to say they had moved my husband and we should head up to the room. As we gathered our things and began to walk out, my son walked over to the gentleman and handed him all his cash. The man said he would be fine and couldn't take the money. My son replied, "We are sorry for your loss and we would like to help you." With tears in his eyes, the man accepted the money.

My son then sat down with the man and led a short prayer. My mom, sister, and I stood there with tears running down our faces. The man came up to thank us. He explained that he flew down to see his 24-year-old sister who had a heart attack and then died this morning. He was not from here and didn't know anyone. He expressed how blessed he was by the compassion, love, and faith in the Lord my son displayed.

I thought about it on the way up to see my husband, and I think we were all open to that opportunity because we had stopped thinking of how scared we were and started thinking of how gratified we were.[15]

That's what the Lord wants for each of us—to live differently because we think of how grateful we are instead of how scared we are.

SO WHAT NOW?

Here are a few specific steps we can take to begin living as more thankful people:

1. Consider the blockades to gratefulness in your life. In this broken world, what factors make gratitude difficult for you? Write down some answers in the space below.

2. Personalize what we've learned. In your own words, list below the positive repercussions of understanding and learning to practice gratitude.

3. Count your blessings. Study after study shows that people who regularly count their blessings live longer, happier, healthier, more productive lives. People who take time to notice and appreciate the good things not only obey the Lord, they live better lives. Count blessings! That changes everything and needs to become part of each person's regular routine. List a few of your blessing below.

CHAPTER 2

OVERCOMING THE ENEMIES OF THANKFULNESS

THEME: It's so hard to remain grateful! Therefore, we must battle the enemies of thanksgiving.

OBJECTIVE: That we overflow with gratitude.

I have a burning question for you: Why are people so often ungrateful? We are. Randy Glasbergen nailed the human race in this cartoon.[16]

"I'm trying to develop an 'attitude of gratitude' but the best I can muster is a 'sentiment of resentment'."

Thanklessness is a demonstrable reality that stretches across all human boundaries. But for some time I have wondered *why*.

Years ago, I served with a ministry at an awesome camp in Germany. The people of Germany blessed me greatly and I loved working very hard with them. But it was strange how rarely I heard "thank you." True, I was dealing mainly with non-Christians, but *vielen dank* was rarely spoken.

Back in America's heartland, I served a couple of summers as a lifeguard at a large waterpark. I performed 28 serious in-water rescues and thousands of pull-outs—lifting people up the sides and out of the crashing waves. In all those rescues, I remember being thanked twice. Two times. Jesus at least had a 10% gratitude expression rate with His lepers. [See Luke 17.] My lifeguard appreciation rate was just over 7%.

One night I was blessed to have supper with a pastor from tribal Africa. His church was so far out in the bush that they weren't on any maps. Through our translator I asked him all about his ministry. His number one problem? Lack of gratitude. Not long after becoming Christians, his congregants began to take God, the scriptures, and this pastor for granted—and he couldn't figure out why. I've heard the same thing from pastors in Mongolia, Nepal, Kazakhstan, Venezuela, Panama, South Africa, Britain, and Russia.

This may astonish you, but I have even heard the same kind of thanklessness from Christians who are being severely persecuted. That seems counter to what we would assume, but it's been my experience. No matter how hounded or secure, rich or poor, slave or free, human beings really struggle with gratitude.

What I wanted to know was *why*. Why are people by and large so graceless and unappreciative? So, I put a little thought into this. I searched scripture, read a lot, and prayed. The summary of what I've learned became this chapter detailing the enemies of gratitude.

THE ENEMIES OF GRATITUDE

The first culprit is *sin*. The Bible depicts this in the fascinating song we call Psalm 140. David wrote this psalm while hiding from Saul. David was hiding in this cave at the time—a rare sandstone cave in Israel. [Photo by author] David was pretty safe here, though his men and supplies were a little cramped in the warrens of passages that scroll through the stone.

David wrote a few songs in this period of his life and they are interestingly different from the bulk of his writing in one way—the "On the run  from Saul" album boasts more sarcasm than usual for him. The sarcasm is subtle and ironic, showing David's great skill in writing. For example, consider the last verse in Psalm 140: "Surely the righteous will give thanks to Your name; The upright will dwell in Your presence." (Psalm 140:13 NASB)

We know that is a sarcastic statement of irony because there are none who are righteous in themselves. There are none who can dwell in God's presence. None. Period. As David says in another song:

> The LORD has looked down from heaven upon the sons of men
> To see if there are any who understand,
> Who seek after God.
> They have all turned aside, together they have become corrupt;
> There is no one who does good, not even one.
> (Psalm 14:2-3 NASB)

The same truth is spoken by other people we consider incredibly holy. Moses had to be hidden from God's presence. Moses! They only guy who spoke to the Father face to face the way a man speaks to his friend! Yet Moses was so unrighteous that God had to hide him in the cleft of the rock. Isaiah—the amazingly wise and faithful Isaiah – he knew that on his own he was unworthy, in his memorable phrase: "a man of unclean lips dwelling among a people of unclean lips." (Isaiah 6:5)

And what reason did Moses and Isaiah give for this inability to dwell with the Most High? Sin. In a word, sin is the problem. All are tainted by sin. Therefore, it stands to reason that no one naturally gives thanks either. Remember, Hebrew poetry is built on parallelism. Thus, the structure is purposefully arranged to illustrate David's powerful, subtle point in Psalm 140.

Just as no one is upright and worthy to dwell in God's presence; so no one is righteous and really lives a life of appropriate gratitude. Can't you imagine what David's feeling? The king he has served so faithfully...the father of David's best friend...the guy David soothed with music...the leader David saved when Goliath threatened...this guy is not seeking David's life to *thank* him! Saul wants to kill David! The righteous give thanks. As David knows from his own soul and the experience with Saul, no person is righteous. Because of sin, no one naturally is grateful.

PRIDE

Sin is the problem, and sin has a number of particular manifestations that are enemies of gratitude. Possibly the most significant is *pride*. Listen to Jesus' searing indictment of pride in Revelation 3:

> For you say, I am rich, I have prospered, and I need nothing, not realizing that you are wretched, pitiable, poor, blind, and naked. I counsel you to buy from me gold refined by fire, so that you may be rich, and white garments so that you may clothe yourself and the shame of your nakedness may not be seen, and salve to anoint your eyes, so that you may see. Those whom I love, I reprove and discipline, so be zealous and repent. (Revelation 3:17-19 ESV)

The city being addressed here was Laodicea, a beautiful and wealthy town just recently being uncovered from over 1000 years of accumulated dirt. Together with a bunch of important cities like Hieropolis and Colossae, Laodicea was a powerful center of land trade in the first century. They had hot and cold running water, modern plumbing, excellent theatres, and universities. In a word, these towns had arrived—or so they thought.

In actuality, they were very needy—as are all people. What they really needed was to see God's truth and His blessings. What they needed was to become grateful instead of thinking they had arrived.

Thank goodness, *we're* not like that! We never sit back in pride and forget to be thankful to the God who alone covers all our needs! But we do, don't we? From wherever we come, with whatever little or much we have, we have an inveterate tendency to become prideful. And that's tragic, because thanksgiving and pride are mutually exclusive.

ENTITLEMENT

The same thing goes for pride's cousin *entitlement*. The *Wall Street Journal's* Diana Kapp tipped me off to a remarkable study published in *Personality and Social Psychology Bulletin*. The investigators tried to come up with a way to measure entitlement.

They tracked attitude surveys from 355,000 high school seniors from the thirty-year period from 1976 to 2007.

- They discovered that desire for lots of money has increased markedly since the survey began in the mid-1970s. The first three years of the survey [1976-1978], only 48% of students thought it was important to have lots of money and nice things. The last three years [2005-2007] a whopping 62% said that was important.

- Meanwhile, willingness to work hard to earn those things has decreased. The early years of the survey, 25% of the High School students admitted that they didn't want to work hard. By the late 1990s, that number climbed to 39%, where it has remained ever since.

- Study coauthors Drs. Jean Twenge and Tim Kasser call this difference a "fantasy gap." They say it is driven by a current culture of narcissism and entitlement.[17]

They are correct. However, this is not something new. The problem of entitlement is age old. Proverbs 21 was penned about 3000 years ago, but reads like today's latest study. Look at this couplet:

> The desire of the sluggard kills him,
> for his hands refuse to labor. (Proverbs 21:25 ESV)

That's entitlement. And it kills. Of course, an entitlement fantasy gap doesn't just kill lives—the point of Proverbs 21:25. It also kills relationships, particularly by destroying gratitude. Likely we have all seen this in action. For example, I know many teenagers who think they are entitled every night to a hot meal made by someone else and prepared exactly to the young person's taste. If such is a student's expectation, will he show thankfulness? No, he won't. A family with such a teenager houses an ungrateful monster.

Of course, that entitlement has usually been carefully if unwittingly coddled by the parents. When the child was little and the parents adjusted the menu every night just to accommodate her ever-changing, amazingly limited palate, what did they teach? That the child was entitled to exactly what she would like every time. We make our monsters through entitlement training.

This occurs in peer relationships as well. Often people who are dating will say to each other, "You deserve to never be unhappy," or "You should never have cause to cry, sweetheart." In reality, such well-intentioned sentiment is harmful horse manure. Since the Garden of Eden, there has never been a successful relationship that was void of tears.

Our job in relationships is not to make anybody happy. Our job is to serve Jesus by serving the other person fully. Such service will surely at some point involve the tears that are part of life's journey this side of heaven. We must learn that no one is entitled to tear-free living. And until one learns that, lack of thanksgiving abounds. This is part of the reason divorce rates are so high. A person cannot be entitled and grateful. And without gratitude, a relationship is in serious trouble.

BITTERNESS

Sometimes expectations devolve into *bitterness,* which is another serious threat to gratitude. Have you ever interacted with a bitter person? If so, you surely noticed the lack of appreciation emanating from them. Bitterness kills thankfulness. You likely also felt the effect the other person's bitterness had on you. Usually, one's sense of gratitude lowers because of an encounter with a bitter person, because bitterness is incredibly contagious. It's almost like fear in that sense. Bitterness spreads. This reality provoked God to give this serious warning: "See to it that no one comes short of the grace of God; that no root of bitterness springing up causes trouble, and by it many be defiled." (Hebrews 12:15 NASB)

Bitterness defiles. It spreads like poison ivy. The reason directors shoot zombie movies instead of bitterness movies is that a bitterness film would be too scary. One of the things that concerns me for my own soul is that I not become a bitter, grumpy old man. Years ago, a wise older gentleman warned me about old age, saying:

> Wayne, getting really old is like being sick. Everything hurts all the time and you don't feel like yourself. And you can't just work harder and fix it because you don't have the energy. So if you want to know what kind of old guy you'll be, ask yourself this, "What am I like when I have the flu?"[18]

Oh my goodness! That terrifies me because I am possibly the biggest whiny brat on the planet when I have the flu. I complain. I want people around, but not too close. I want everything I want brought to me before I even express that I want it. Most of all, I'm mad that I'm ill. I get on the edge of bitterness thinking about how God would allow this to happen.

In other words, I am a bitter jerk when I'm sick. And that's a great warning sign that I better get to work uprooting that attitude now, before I experience those pains every day. Gratitude is right and good and makes life joyful. I cannot allow anything to mess with my attitude of gratitude. If I don't get that root of bitterness out of my life, it will corrupt many in God's community.

DISILLUSIONMENT

Disillusionment is our next enemy. It appears to be less contagious than bitterness, although it can become very popular when expressed as a kind of knowing cynicism. Like bitterness, disillusionment harms the redeemed community by leading people away from the Lord. In Jeremiah 18, God describes how hopeless disillusionment causes humans to turn away from Him, saying: "And they said, 'There is no hope: but we will walk after our own devices, and we will every one do the imagination of his evil heart.'" (Jeremiah 18:12 KJV)

Times were tough in Jeremiah 18! But the prophet was calling for people to give thanks and trust the Lord. He promised that God would see His community through the dangers of the age. But they refused to follow. Such is always the case with the disillusioned cynic. Rather than trusting God and submitting to Him in gratitude, the defeated person runs off into deadening foolishness. In fact, the only creativity found in the disillusioned person is "the imagination of his evil heart."

We should also notice the fatalism in the passage. It's an ironic truth that some people resent God's sovereignty, wrongly calling it fatalism. Fascinatingly, they are the people most likely to live in a fatalistic manner, driven by hopeless disillusion. People ignore the goodness of God and His statutes. Instead, we dive into a hopeless thought pattern that has no appreciation for the Lord. We follow our own path, that in reality lacks all originality, no matter how often we sing "I did it my way." And the end result is always disappointed disillusionment.

I see this often when I work with students. As a college professor, I have noticed some very encouraging news of late. Most edifying is that the work ethic of students today is generally impressive. I have taught and graded at undergrad and graduate levels for years and am happy to testify that many of the students of today really do work hard. I know there is much evidence to the contrary, but in my experience the 21st century student is willing to put forth real effort.

However, I have also noted a very disheartening trend among those I teach. Today's students are a pretty cynical bunch. At least in my experience, they are very quick to become disillusioned. They remind me of newspaper reporters as depicted in old movies—cynical and hopeless even as they work hard to bang out lots of copy on their typewriters.

Sadly, such disillusionment eventually wears them down. Students become depressed; their work suffers; and worst of all, they lose the attitude of gratitude that could give them needed perspective. That scenario can easily spiral into our next enemy.

DISCOURAGED ISOLATION
Discouraged isolation can be devastating.

> My soul is in the midst of lions;
> I lie down amid fiery beasts—
> the children of man, whose teeth are spears and arrows,
> whose tongues are sharp swords. (Psalm 57:4 ESV)

These words come from another great poem written by David while hiding in a cave—possibly the same cave as Psalm 140. David is understandably discouraged. Though surrounded by his fighters, he feels separated from good people. He feels alone.

The introduction to the psalm points this out, instructing: "For the choir director; set to Al-tashheth. A Mikhtam of David, when he fled from Saul in the cave." (NASB) I do not know the tune for Al-tasheth, but the word means "do not destroy." Some tune called "do not destroy" had become so famous that David wrote new lyrics to that tune. Thus, David was the first "Weird Al" Yankovik [a performer who became famous rewriting lyrics to popular songs]. David took the tune from "We are the champions" and wrote a new song to it.

This new song was a *mikhtam* [meekh tom']. No one really knows what that word means. However, it appears six times in Hebrew literature and it's always connected to a song of struggle or lament. Interestingly, the word itself comes from engraving on metal. It's a verb that meant to etch something deeply and permanently.

So, this song is a deeply etched lesson David learned while on the run for his life. And it's lacking in gratitude, as one might expect. Look again at the wretched attitude in verse 4:

> My soul is in the midst of lions;
> I lie down amid fiery beasts—
> the children of man, whose teeth are spears and arrows,
> whose tongues are sharp swords. (Psalm 57:4 ESV)

In his discouraged isolation, David sees his companions as only "worthless fellows." He compares them to dragons and violent lions. We know from other passages that these guys were tough and bloody mercenaries, so David's not completely misguided in his assessment. However, we also know that these are mighty men gathered around David, faithful warriors willing to do anything for him. Other texts show that these are valorous, lean, fighting machines. Why can't David see that side of things as well?

In verse 4 that more complete understanding is missing because he's beaten down by discouraged isolation. And discouraged isolation is just like disillusionment, bitterness, entitlement, pride, and all sin—it keeps us from the gratitude that changes everything.

DEFEATING THE ENEMIES

Are you depressed yet? Don't be! Because we are now going to get to the good stuff about defeating the enemies of thanksgiving. Here's a great first step to victory—*consider God's character and works.*

That's exactly what David does next. Look at the very following verses in Psalm 57:

> Be exalted, O God, above the heavens!
> Let your glory be over all the earth!
> They set a net for my steps;
> my soul was bowed down.
> They dug a pit in my way,
> but they have fallen into it themselves. *Selah*
> My heart is steadfast, O God,
> my heart is steadfast!
> I will sing and make melody! (Psalm 57:5-7 ESV)

David does some hard thinking here in the cave, huddled at night with the smelly mighty men all around him. He starts remembering what he knows. He knows that God causes all to work for the good of His people. He knows that every tragedy has a purpose. He even remembers that God will ultimately catch every person in his or her own sin. The one who set traps for others will be trapped himself.

And that wakes up something in David's heart. These ruminations on the long purposes and sure hand of God cause David to start giving thanks. See it there in the last three lines? Suddenly the cave is not so dark. Suddenly David is looking out at the wide world. Thinking about God's character has birthed real thanksgiving.

Another David, David Wade, a member of my pulpit team, sent me a great note on this:

> I have frequently heard the question, "How can I give thanks when (fill in the blank) is happening to me or to someone I love?" J. I. Packer gave one of the best answers I've heard when he says, [from p. 82 of Packer's *Evangelism and the Sovereignty of God*] "One day we shall see that nothing – literally nothing—which could have increased our eternal happiness has been denied us, and that nothing – literally nothing—that could have reduced that happiness has been left with us."[19]

When I consider God's character, I cannot help but be transported into the missing and needed spirit of thanksgiving. That doesn't mean I stop crying out in my pain! God cares about that pain and the Bible says that He weeps with me. He wants me to hurt with Him. But even as I lament, I give thanks. I know it sounds odd, but it isn't strange when you are really in that place. In fact, it seems the most right and natural thing in the world to be crying with my eyes even as my heart is thanking God who gives and takes away for good.

This is what Paul is getting at in his pithy, staccato commands from God in 1 Thessalonians 5:

> Rejoice always;
> pray without ceasing;
> in everything give thanks; for this is God's will for you in Christ Jesus. (1 Thessalonians 5:16-18 NASB)

Those are not disjointed instructions. They actually go together. I rejoice, I give thanks all the time, even as I share my continual needs with God. The two things are very much connected – my continuous ache this side of heaven and my continuous delight that in Jesus Christ I have every reason for gratitude!

Have you ever faced an extremely painful battle and gone to God in serious prayer about it? I have as well, many times. I am occasionally blessed with mail from people going through such struggles, and in their letters I hear the same glorious truths David shares in Psalm 57. For example, one man recently wrote me:

> I was really having it out with God, seriously hurting, you know what I mean? And as I stayed engaged in that conversation [note: like David's *steadfast* comment in Psalm 57:7] something happened. I don't know how to describe it. The circumstances were the same, but I could sense the hand of God in it all. It was incredible. Even as I kept crying, my tears were for joy as much as sorrow.[20]

HONESTLY CONSIDER MY OWN CHARACTER AND WORKS

If we are going to defeat these enemies, Iwe must consider God's character. We also need to honestly consider our own character and works. There are many brilliant examples of this in the Bible, but I am drawn to the crucifixion scene recorded in Luke 23:

> One of the criminals who were hanged *there* was hurling abuse at Him, saying, "Are You not the Christ? Save Yourself and us!"
>
> But the other answered, and rebuking him said, "Do you not even fear God, since you are under the same sentence of condemnation? And we indeed *are suffering* justly, for we are receiving what we deserve for our deeds; but this man has done nothing wrong."
> And he was saying, "Jesus, remember me when You come in Your kingdom!"
>
> And He said to him, "Truly I say to you, today you shall be with Me in Paradise." (Luke 23:39-43 NASB)

This speech by a thief on a cross utterly dethrones my entitlement tendencies. This guy had every reason to be whiny. He was in excruciating pain; yet, he recognized that his own character made self-justification impossible. He cried out for a relationship with Jesus that was all by grace.

In the past week, how many times do you think you have heard "You deserve!" Whether an advertisement or your own voice, how many times has your brain been bombarded with "I deserve (fill in the blank)?" If you are like most people, the answer numbers in the dozens. Dozens of times each week we rationalize the lie that we *deserve*.

Let's kill off that infectious lie with a healthy injection of truth. Remember what we learned earlier from David? Look again at Psalm 14:

> The LORD has looked down from heaven upon the sons of men
> To see if there are any who understand,
> Who seek after God.
> They have all turned aside, together they have become corrupt;
> There is no one who does good, not even one.
> (Psalm 14:2-3 NASB)

In the New Testament, God continues to develop the thought, communicating in the book of Romans: "For all have sinned and fall short of the glory of God" and "the wages of sin is death." (Romans 3:23 and 6:23a ESV) The reality is that my character and works are both tainted with sin. And that earns me death. Period. I deserve eternal separation from life and from the God who gives life. All humans deserve nothing. Period.

I was chosen for a jury selection room once. I was potential juror #4, so it was almost certain I would be seated on the jury. The defense attorney got up and began her important work of setting the stage to defend her client. But she was really irritating in her continual assertion of "rights." She kept railing on about what her client *deserved*.

Finally, she began to question the jurors. She turned to me first, and said, "Dr. Braudrick, as a biblical Christian you can surely agree that my client deserves the benefit of the doubt." I laughed and said, "Not hardly! As a biblical Christian, I know he deserves what I deserve—death as a person separated from God."

I was not seated on that jury. In fact, I was asked to go home. I hope the client did well and got a fair trial. But I more fervently hope that he used the opportunity to examine his soul and discover what honest introspection always teaches—that we deserve nothing.

If that were the end of the story, the Bible would be just another sad tale, like something Hemingway would write while suffering with a hangover. Thankfully, there is a huge "but" in verse 23 of Romans 6. Look at the entire verse: "For the wages of sin is death, but the free gift of God is eternal life in Christ Jesus our Lord." (Romans 6:23 ESV)

God has not left humans to our deserved fate. He has given us reason for eternal thanksgiving because He has shown us His grace in Jesus!

ACT ON THE TRUTH OF GOD'S GRACE.

So, how can one defeat the enemies of gratitude? Consider God; consider self; and then act on the marvelous blessing of God's grace. Paul's letter to the Colossians has much to say on this:

> Therefore as you have received Christ Jesus the Lord, *so* walk in Him, having been firmly rooted *and now* being built up in Him and established in your faith, just as you were instructed, *and* overflowing with gratitude. (Colossians 2:6-7 NASB)

We discussed this text in the first chapter, but I want to note one more thing. Look at all the action verbs here: received, walk, rooted, built, established, instructed, overflowing. Most of these verbs are describing what God has done: He rooted you in Jesus…He builds you up…He establishes you in your trust…He gets you instruction.

In response, the Christian's role is to receive…walk…and overflow with gratitude. Because of what God has done and is doing, we can do what God wants done. We can act on His truth, which will inevitably lead to thanksgiving. God wants us to live out this awesome life He has granted in Jesus and He knows that it is best for us to live that out in overflowing gratitude.

One of those wonderful people with whom I worked in Germany is named Pascal. He is now a successful and award-winning filmmaker. A few weeks ago, I got a note from Pascal attached to this photo. He said:

I'm currently in the middle of the Bolivian jungle filming a part of a documentary. This film tells the story of Mary, an 83-year-old lady with cerebral palsy. Mary travels the world helping other disabled people. She is so grateful for what God does for her each day that she wants to spread the love and give others reason to praise the Lord. (Oh, by the way

she just got married 3 months ago—how's that for a reality check for how you're living your life?)

Anyway we're in Trinidad, Bolivia today, where Mary and a team of volunteers are distributing wheel chairs. The father in this photo walks in with his 9-year-old handicapped son in his arms. He's carried him to the distribution center through pouring rain, just to help his child by getting him his very own first wheel chair ever. You should have seen the smile on the kid's face—and on Mary's!

I grabbed this image as father and son were walking back home in the rain, thankful and happy.[21]

If I want to defeat the lethargy of disillusion, the absurdity of pride, or any of the other enemies, I need to give thanks because of what my gracious God has done and continues to do! Christians have been writing about this for two millennia. Regardless of their persecution or other difficulties, our forefathers learned that real victory is found in acting on God's truth instead of the shifting feelings or attitudes of humanity. Our forebears in Christ learned that gratitude is life changing. As Justin Martyr wrote in the 2nd century, "Wherefore we give thanks no matter what because of God's blessedness to us."[22]

An early martyr wrote those words as he saw persecution bearing down on him and other Christians. One of my favorite modern expressions of this came about a generation ago. Christian writers

Brown Bannister and Michael Vincent Hudson penned a great poem about gratitude:

> Praise the Lord!
> He can work through those who praise Him.
> Praise the Lord!
> For our God inhabits praise.
> Praise the Lord!
> For the chains that seem to bind you
> Serve only to remind you
> That they drop powerless behind you
> When you praise Him.[23]

In Colossians 3, the Apostle Paul writes:

> Let the word of Christ richly dwell within you, with all wisdom teaching and admonishing one another with psalms *and* hymns *and* spiritual songs, singing with thankfulness in your hearts to God. Whatever you do in word or deed, *do* all in the name of the Lord Jesus, giving thanks through Him to God the Father. (Colossians 3:16-17 NASB)

Paul really fleshes it out here. Act on God's truth. Let God's Word work so strongly in you that you overcome the enemies of thanksgiving. In my office where I currently am writing, there are multiple copies of A. A. Milne's Winnie the Pooh books. Knowing I am a fan of his beautiful writing, friends have given me copies in English, Spanish, Russian, and Latin. [Yes, Latin! *Winnie Ille Pu*] I think Mr. Milne brilliantly summarized Paul's Colossians idea. He wrote, "Piglet noticed that even though he had a very small heart, it could hold a rather large amount of gratitude."

OK, let's put this all together. When we were kids, many of us learned a little life-saving poem:

> Stop, look, and listen before you cross the street.
> Use your eyes. Use your ears. And then use your feet.

A Benedictine monk named David Steindl-Rast wrote a book [*Gratefulness, the Heart of Prayer*] in which he claims that childhood poem applies to defeating the enemies of gratefulness. Now much of Friar David's book is biblically rather sketchy, but this idea is sound. When we stop, look, and listen, it changes everything.

We slow down and really consider God's character and work. We do the same with our own hearts. We use our eyes and ears. And then, filled with gratitude that we who deserve nothing have so much—including a forever relationship with God Himself—then we use our feet. We act in gratitude. We act on God's truth.

SO WHAT NOW?

1. Think about the character of God as revealed in the Bible. Write some of His attributes in the space below.

2. Prayerfully ask the Lord to reveal entitlement in your heart. Thank Him for His undeserved merit that comes through the sacrifice of Jesus. If you have never done so, trust Jesus as Savior. Believe on Him who died for you and conquered the grave so that you might follow Him in everlasting life.

3. Stop, look, and listen—then use your feet to cross the street into thankfulness. List some ways you can live out your gratefulness.

CHAPTER 3

LIVE WITH A GENUINE ATTITUDE OF GRATITUDE

THEME: There are two great keys to avoiding the defeated cynicism and bitterness of the typical life: respond to God's call and live in light of *hesed*.

OBJECTIVE: That we live as called, grateful children of God.

Have you ever seen a sinkhole? Sinkholes occur when a gap appears in the ground beneath the surface. Usually it's because an underground river or aquifer has run dry or been diverted. Acidification because of limestone soils also plays a role because the more acidic lime water eats holes in the rock beneath.[24]

When that happens, the unseen ground underneath experiences a cavernous emptiness. It's all dry and terribly unstable, though no one on the surface knows anything about it. Then, at some point the surface collapses into the empty space. Ironically, this usually happens when it rains really hard. Isn't that odd? But water is very heavy, and the flooding water seeps down, eroding the dry structure underneath.

By the way, Florida has the perfect combination of underground rivers, lots of rain, and limestone soils and thus Florida has many large sinkholes. Missouri and Texas are also known for sinkholes.

Years ago, I was on an advisory board of a ministry headed by Gordon MacDonald. Gordon had just written a best-selling book about what he called "the sinkhole syndrome." I think his concept is brilliant. Gordon looked at Scripture and life and realized that:

The majority of humans spend their lives only on the surface. They have accumulated a host of good and perhaps even excellent assets such as academic degrees, work experiences, key relationships, and physical strength or beauty...There is nothing wrong with all that. But often it is discovered too late that the private world of a person...the [inner soul] is in a state of weakness. And when that is true, one is very close to collapsing in the sinkhole syndrome.[25]

As you may know, Jesus claimed that He is Himself the giver of Living Water. John relates the dramatic expression: "On the last day of the feast, the great day, Jesus stood up and cried out, "If anyone thirsts, let him come to me and drink. Whoever believes in me, as the Scripture has said, 'Out of his heart will flow rivers of living water.' Now this he said about the Spirit, whom those who believed in him were to receive, for as yet the Spirit had not been given, because Jesus was not yet glorified." (John 7:37-39 ESV)

The one who trusts in Jesus has ever-bubbling springs in his soul no matter how dry the circumstances of life. Without Jesus, without the relationship with God offered in Christ, a person is empty inside. Gordon's thesis went on to describe how over time even people who have received Jesus as Savior can still dry up. It's not that they become unjustified or un-born again. That's biblically absurd.

They just stop going to the well. They stop actively trusting Jesus. They let the living water get diverted. They get absorbed in all the surface issues that consume our days. Christians can even do this through their efforts to follow Jesus in spiritual life! I'm serious. We can become dried-up sinkholes waiting to happen, even as we work hard on being mature followers of Jesus. This is why Paul would write the churches in

Galatia—and all of us—"How foolish can you be? After starting your new lives in the Spirit, why are you now trying to become perfect by your own human effort?" (Galatians 3:3 NLT)

The Bible is full of these stories. So is every pastor's counseling file. Hard-working, well-intentioned people dry up with no inner spiritual living water. Christians forget to draw on the real inner life they have in Father, Jesus, and Spirit. We get fleshly and surface about everything, including our Christian walk. And that means we become a sinkhole waiting to happen.

Such was Gordon's thesis, a fantastic summary of a scriptural reality. Sadly, it also became his own story. Rev. MacDonald made national headlines when he was caught in adultery. He was shown to be a liar and manipulator of the highest caliber. It was an awful time, especially for Gordon's family and for the board on which I served.

But it was also a great season. Gordon humbled himself. He went through a restoration process, and has seen the Lord rebuild his life mightily. While I have some concerns with the process of Gordon's restoration, I am thrilled with the result—especially the fact that he and Gail have celebrated their 50th wedding anniversary.

Here's the point: if a spiritual leader like Gordon MacDonald can find himself at the bottom of a sinkhole…if biblical heroes like David can see their inner world collapse…then you and I are not immune. I'm thrilled that Gordon, David, and many others have been rebuilt. But our goal is to make sure you and I never collapse in the first place!

To live in a way that the living water is always our support, we should master two principles: 1) living as people who are called, not driven; and 2) learn to gratefully meditate on God's *hesed* [a term we'll explain below.]

BE CALLED, NOT DRIVEN.

> Blessed *be* the God and Father of our Lord Jesus Christ, who has blessed us with every spiritual blessing in the heavenly *places* in Christ, just as He chose us in Him before the foundation of the world, that we would be holy and blameless before Him. In love He predestined us to adoption as

sons through Jesus Christ to Himself, according to the kind intention of His will, to the praise of the glory of His grace, which He freely bestowed on us in the Beloved...*I pray that the eyes of your heart may be enlightened, so that you will know what is the hope of His calling, what are the riches of the glory of His inheritance in the saints, and what is the surpassing greatness of His power toward us who believe.* (Ephesians 1:3-6; 18-19a NASB)

See the apostle's prayer request? Paul's deep desire for each Christian is that we'd experience *opens eyes to God's calling*. Up on the surface, life is all about being driven. We are herded and/or herding people and things. We push. We labor. We fight ahead. And that's not all bad. Indeed, it's part of life since Adam left the Garden.

But it's not enough! Being driven is empty. It's hollow. It never really arrives. It lacks joy, peace, and gratitude. That's why driven people can't ever enjoy any victory. It's why they don't ever really rest. God calls us to open our eyes, to unstop our ears, to recognize the greatness of the fact that He has *called* us. The first step in stopping the sinkhole is to be called, not driven. And that presupposes that we recognize God's effectual and effective calling.

Imagine that your phone rings. You look to see who's calling. It's the coolest guy in the world. You can't believe it! You think, "This must be a wrong number!" But still you answer the phone. Right?

With that in mind, look again at the Ephesians text above. God chose you. He purposefully calls you. The coolest, most incredible Being called you. Open your eyes. You didn't find God. He sought you.

Some of my friends have experienced an earthly expression of this via adoption. They have seen the power of parents who seek out a kiddo and call that child their own. John relates that to every believer in Jesus, saying: "See what love the Father has given us, that we should be called children of God; and that is what we are." (1 John 3:1 NRSV)

John, like Paul, wants us to open our eyes to the calling of God. Not the driving; the calling. But it's not always easy to abide in love, is it? I have known many adoptive families that struggled mightily—mainly because the adopted kiddo just wouldn't open his eyes to the unconditional calling of the parents. Wanting to guard his heart, the adopted child fights against rejection he feels certain will be coming. He sometimes even acts out to precipitate the situation to more quickly get over a separation that seems to his mind inevitable.

God, like all great parents, won't let that separation happen. He won't reject His own. He wants His people to open their eyes to His calling. It's a critical part of enjoying a real depth of life under the surface.

RELY ON GOD AS YOU WORK.

Another part of living as *called, not driven* is found in passages like this:

> Between the city walls, you build a reservoir
> for water from the old pool.
> But you never ask for help from the One who did all this.
> You never considered the One who planned this long ago.
> (Isaiah 22:11 NLT)

The point is to rely on God as you work. That's what Israel didn't do here. The context is the hard work of preparing Jerusalem against invaders from the north and east. The people did lots of good work, but didn't do the only *critical* thing. They didn't make sure that all their efforts were performed out of a complete reliance on the Lord.

The phraseology is telling. God is really the One who accomplishes all that concerns His people—even when He uses them to do the work. God made all these plans before Jerusalem even existed. To operate outside of engagement with Him is like building a building without any plans. It's ridiculous. In fact, Isaiah 22 calls this lack of reliance on God a defeat in "the valley of vision." One can't see rightly to find victory if one is not resting in the Lord through all efforts.

Our Puritan forefathers were very taken with this concept. They discussed the "valley of vision" a lot, and called for humble seeking of God in every part of life. Those doughty Puritans worked hard. They began an amazing country in America greatly because they knew that real vision comes by humbly relying on God.[26] If we are called, we stay engaged with the caller. We rely on him even as we work. By contrast, when we are driven our work becomes our all and we lack depth. This is especially seen when tragedy or crises arise.

Stanley Jones was a missionary to India in the 20th century. After many years of great and very popular ministry, he had a stroke that left him unable to speak or eat for a time. Nonetheless, he fought back through therapy—and did it by God's strength. In his convalescence, Jones began to see how *little* people rely on God. Look at what he wrote in his book *The Divine Yes:*

> I was talking to a bishop who had retired. He was frustrated. When he was no longer in the limelight...he was frustrated and told me so. He wanted to know the secret of victorious living. I told him it was in self-surrender. The difference was in giving the innermost self to Jesus... When the outer strands of [his life] were broken by retirement, the inner strands were not enough to hold him... Fortunately, with me, surrender to Jesus was the primary thing, and when the outer strands were cut by this stroke, my life didn't shake.[27]

Want to avoid a sinkhole in retirement or tragedy? Surrender all to Jesus. Even as you work hard, surrender all to God. After all, God has called us! We are not driven, we are <u>called</u>.

SEE GOD EVER-INCREASE IN YOUR LIFE.

Because we are called according to God's great purpose, Christians can enjoy the same attitude of John the Baptizer: "The one who has the bride is the bridegroom. The friend of the bridegroom, who stands and hears him, rejoices greatly at the bridegroom's voice. Therefore this joy of mine is now complete. He must increase, but I must decrease." (John 3:29-30 ESV) John the Baptizer is drinking deeply of the living water. He recognizes here the most important two facts of theology: 1) There is a Messiah. 2) I am not He.

John sees something very critical that at this point is missed by both John's followers and those flocking to Jesus—God can and must increase in your life if you wish to have fullness of joy. This isn't a quantity issue. It's a quality phenomenon. I can find increasing joy by continual surrender, whereby I see God ever-increase in my life.

Here in the United States, we drive our large herds of cattle from behind. I grew up where cowboys were basically worshipped and every kid learned to ride a cutting horse in order to drive cattle. And that's wonderful. But studying in Israel I learned something fascinating. Animals there are not driven. They are called. The shepherd walks in front of the animals and calls them—and the sheep learn to follow.

In fact, the wisest sheep learn to follow closer and closer, letting the shepherd fill more and more of their vision. That shepherd takes care of the animals. That shepherd takes them to water and food. Ram or lamb, the smart ones see the shepherd closer and closer.

This kind of response to God's calling—this drawing ever closer—changes a person from the inside out. It makes for a soul that is led by the Lord. It makes for a soul that stands strong through all storms, just as Jesus predicted for any who act on His Words. To keep from imploding, follow Jesus. Surrender your will to follow the Good Shepherd. See Him ever-increase in your life. As Jesus said, "When he puts forth all his own, he goes ahead of them, and the sheep follow him because they know his voice." (John 10:4 NASB)

Being called is critical if we are going to avoid the sinkhole syndrome. It makes for true internal strength. The sixth president of the United States, John Quincy Adams, thought this the most important quality in a person. President Adams wrote to his daughter Dorothy about what she should look for in a husband, saying: "Regard the honor and moral character of the man more than all other circumstances. Think of no other greatness but that of the soul, no other riches but those of the heart."[28]

Now, I know what you're likely thinking. At this point in the chapter, you are asking, "So. Pastor. This is all very nice about avoiding sinkholes. But what does that have to do with a *gratitude* series? You are supposed to be teaching on *gratitude* for goodness sake!"

GRATEFULLY MEDITATE ON GOD'S *HESED*.

Thank you for asking. The answer to your question is found in the second great scriptural principle that prevents sinkholes—gratitude.

Specifically, the Bible teaches us to gratefully meditate on God's *hesed*. Psalm 136 is a great example:

> Give thanks to the Lord, for He is good,
> For His lovingkindness is everlasting.
> Give thanks to the God of gods,
> For His lovingkindness is everlasting.
> Give thanks to the Lord of lords,
> For His lovingkindness is everlasting.
> To Him who alone does great wonders,
> For His lovingkindness is everlasting.
> (Psalm 136:1-4 NASB)

The song goes on to discuss God's work in creation, in the history of Israel, and in providing for each person. It ends with this statement: "Give thanks to the God of heaven, For His lovingkindness is everlasting." (Psalm 136:26 NASB) That refrain runs through all 26 couplets of the song. "For His lovingkindness is everlasting."

And the psalm is bookended by the parallel statements of gratitude:

> Give thanks to the Lord, for He is good,
> For His lovingkindness is everlasting. (verse 1)
> Give thanks to the God of heaven,
> For His lovingkindness is everlasting. (verse 26)

Give thanks! Show gratitude! Why? Because God is God of heaven. He is the Lord. And He is good. And that is coupled with the main idea, the oft-repeated refrain: His lovingkindness endures forever. Lovingkindness is an amazingly beautiful Hebrew word transliterated *hesed* [hae' sed]. *Hesed* means "loyal love." Specifically, it refers to unshakeable love—the covenant love of God who will keep His Word and will keep His people.

And this *hesed* of God lasts how long? Forever.

Psalm 136 calls for us to gratefully meditate on this, to look at all of life and all of history and consider God's *hesed*. This is life changing, friends! It not only shores you up against a soul implosion, it broadens and deepens all of life. In this text, there are illuminations regarding how this works in real life. I suggest you study Psalm 136 and think through them all, but for this space I'll limit the discussion to a few that have changed me.

COME TO YOUR SENSES.

First, come to your senses. Look, listen, taste, smell, hear. The Psalmist describes God's love in sensory terms. "To Him who made *the* great lights, For His lovingkindness is everlasting; Who gives food to all flesh, For His lovingkindness is everlasting." (Psalm 136:7, 25 NASB) God made the sun and the moon as reflections of His covenant love. Look at them. Observe. Think, says the psalmist. He also deals with smell and taste. Meditate on the manifold sensory blessing of God.

By the way, this is another indication of how biblical meditation differs from the nonsense of eastern meditation. Biblical meditation is all about filling your head with God's Word and works. Eastern meditation is conversely about emptying. It's about overriding or shutting down senses and input—the opposite of God's calling. Why do you think the English word "nonsense" has the meaning it does? Because shutting down your senses is idiotic. It frankly is demonic. The Bible calls for one to come to one's senses and thus be filled, not emptied.

Specifically, we are to open our eyes and use our minds so we can be filled with gratitude for the manifold *hesed* of God. This explains why Psalm 19 shouts:

> The heavens are telling of the glory of God;
> And their expanse is declaring the work of His hands.
> Day to day pours forth speech,
> And night to night reveals knowledge.
> (Psalm 19:1-2 NASB)

All of creation sings about God's incredible love and skill. Look…really look at what God does. For example, pull up on your phone or computer an image of the Aurora Australis (Southern Lights). Stunning, isn't it? God incredibly uses magnetic fields, static electricity, light waves and more to create dancing curtains in the sky!

Look! And look into God's Word—the other and more precise form of revelation. Psalm 19 continues so beautifully:

> The law of the Lord is perfect,
> reviving the soul;
> the testimony of the Lord is sure,
> making wise the simple;
> the precepts of the Lord are right,
> rejoicing the heart;
> the commandment of the Lord is pure,
> enlightening the eyes. (Psalm 19:7-8 ESV)

God's *hesed* is everlasting. Come to your senses and meditate on this. It revives your soul; makes you wise; gives joy; and enlightens.

DEVELOP A HEAD FOR HISTORY.

Another part of meditating on God's *hesed* involves developing a head for history. I really enjoy the study of history; in fact, history was the basis of my first degree. But one needn't have a passion for history like mine. You just need to understand it and look through it. Thus, Psalm 136 continues:

> To Him who divided the Red Sea asunder,
> For His lovingkindness is everlasting,
> And made Israel pass through the midst of it,
> For His lovingkindness is everlasting;
> But He overthrew Pharaoh and his army in the Red Sea,
> For His lovingkindness is everlasting.
> (Psalm 136:13-15 NASB)

That pithily describes the famous moment when Israel passed through water that swamped the pursuing Egyptians. Millions of Jews were spared so that God's people could be free and His plan wouldgo forward. The oppressors of God's people were caught in the very thing they tried to use to trap Israel. This moment changed Israel and all of history forever.

My son recently wrote a poem that captures nicely the meaning of the Red Sea crossing:

> Freed from death's asylum
> Fresh air to breathe again
> The seeds you sow grow right on
> Freedom is yours so go right on
> Run away into another day
> It is a gift of grace
> You live to see another day.[29]

Of course, you could read that history and be thinking, in your favorite Bored Valley Girl voice, "Oh my goodness. Like, that is just so in the past. Why does that even matter <u>at all</u> for my life today?"

Think. God had promised those Hebrews that He would lead them out. He promised to make a free people out of those slaves. And He kept that covenant. His hesed endured. With that in mind, ponder what God has promised you, Christian of the New Covenant. Think of one promise God has made to all believers in Jesus (there are many, just pick one).

Now, will God keep that promise? Will His covenant love last? Yes! How do we know? Because He says so and He has shown that He always keeps His Word. When we develop a head for history we begin to see that it's His story. We are reminded that He always has and always will fulfill His covenants.

Another part of a head for history is, like the Psalmist, noting the way your own past has been guided. Gratitude changes how I live now. And gratitude bubbles up in my heart when I look back on how my own past has been shaped by God.

A friend of mine keeps a fascinating blog in which she examines entries from her own 7th grade journals. That's right. This grown lady looks again at things she wrote as a young Christian woman struggling through the gauntlet of being in middle school. Then she comments on the passages. It's fascinating reading. Here's what impresses me most—everything is clearly exposed as a tool God used to develop His daughter. No matter whether it seemed good or bad at the time, from the perspective of where she is now—an experienced mother of two who walks with Christ each day—from here, she is able to praise God for His *hesed* even when reading the tear-stained pages of a teenage diary.

Occasionally, looking at our own history reminds us that we had better heads when we were young. That's what Jesus was saying to His disciples when He made them look at a small child and told them to "Have the faith of a little child."[30] Sometimes kids are better at meditating on God's *hesed* than adults are. Another poem by my son Michael addresses this:

> I think you would be amazed at what you find
> If you could see life through the eyes of a child
> You would be so grateful for the sunshine
> You would be amazed at how much could make you smile
> With no fear of what may come tomorrow.[31]

How can I gratefully meditate on God's *hesed*? Come to my senses. Develop a head for history. Another method is to *give*. Arthur Brooks addresses this in a compelling article:

> American generosity is internationally exceptional and generally amazes foreigners, especially those from the social democracies across the Atlantic. As a European acquaintance once asked me, "What's in it for you?"
>
> A reasonable question. Leave aside for a moment the metaphysical rewards of giving; as a social scientist would say, they are "empirically untestable." Here in this mortal coil, does giving boost our odds of living longer and healthier lives? Will it make us more attractive? If we fail to donate, will others think we were raised by wolves?
>
> The answer to all these questions is "yes." For starters, happiness and giving are strongly correlated. The University of Chicago's General Social Survey shows that charitable givers are 43% likelier to say they are "very happy" than nongivers. Nongivers are a whopping 3.5 times more likely than givers to say they are "not happy at all."
>
> Skeptics will question the causality here. Does charitable giving make us happier, vice versa or both? Experimental studies hold the answer. In 2008, researchers from Harvard

and the University of British Columbia found that the amount subjects spent on themselves was inconsequential for happiness, while spending on others yielded significant happiness gains.

Giving improves our health, too. In a new study of more than 800 Detroit residents, a psychologist from the University of Buffalo found that volunteering significantly lowers the association between stressful life events and death.[32]

Charitable giving is even good for our looks. In 2009, Dutch and British researchers showed female college students one of three videos featuring the same handsome actor. In the first, he gives generously to a beggar on the street; in the second, he hands over just a little money; and in the third, the man gives nothing. The more he gave, the more handsome he appeared to the women in the study.

As remarkable as all this may seem, these findings meet with scholarly consensus, not controversy. Giving generously to the causes we value really does boost our well-being and our esteem in the eyes of others. Consider the science and ask yourself: Can you really afford not to give?

So, on behalf of my colleagues in America's millions of nonprofits, voluntary organizations and houses of worship, I want you to know we're here for you. We want to help you become healthier, happier and better looking.[33]

That's funny, but the point is true. Give, and you develop a heart that sees God's grace—which is the healthiest thing anyone can do. Same thing can happen when you *keep a journal.*

As we observed with my friend, journaling can help one see the development of blessing out of difficulties. It can expose answered prayer and other blessings that we forget so easily. In response to a journaling assignment, one of my undergraduate students sent me an exemplary story about an Australian named Lynne Scrivens. In 2013 Lynne decided to start being more cognizant of gratitude, so every day of that year she posted to Facebook something for which she was grateful. Beth Greenfield of Yahoo describes the process:

> Early status updates included being grateful for exercise, air conditioning and praise from her boss. She then continued through 2013 by posting about details ranging from those clearly important—an afternoon with her sister, support from her friends during her three-month sobriety commitment, a relative's clean bill of health after a scare—to the seemingly trivial, including a good book, rain boots, a productive day of errands, and front-row seats at a Beyoncé concert.[34]

We've talked about the Scripture and the science so you know that this practice likely had a very positive effect. Lynne's own summary is compelling:

> I'm grateful for this project. I'm grateful for my friends for tolerating it. It's amazing how long I spent each day thinking about what I was grateful for. Did it make a difference? Yes. It forced me to look on the bright side of life, even on crappy days… And I'm heading into 2014 with a great big smile, and for that I'm eternally grateful.[35]

Here's another specific step I highly recommend—*choose a memory tool*. Find something that you regularly encounter and use that encounter as an opportunity to thank God for His covenant love.

I have a friend who gives thanks at every red light when he's in the car and not talking to someone. Doesn't that sound odd, giving thanks at a *red* light? He says no. It's part of how he remembers that he's called and not driven. It has become a regular way for him stop and consider all the blessings he's flown by all day with no thought.

When my kids were infants I made it a practice to give thanks to God every time I changed a diaper. And yes, I changed a lot of diapers because God's men are servants. No matter how noxious the product, I took that opportunity to give thanks.

Yours may be different, but I hope you will develop a gratitude memory trigger. It is an excellent idea to develop a thankful moment each day—when putting on shoes…when logging on to email…when you pick up your purse…pause and thank God.

Do you want to avoid the sinkhole syndrome? Then live as one who is called not driven and give thanks for God's unending love. One way to find out how well we are doing in this is to *watch your language.* Words show what's in the heart. When we use certain words, it shows that we are thinking like a thankful, called child of God.

Look for words like "thank you, gifts, blessed, fortunate, gracious." These are indicative of a heart focused on God's grace. By contrast, "I, mine, deserve, rights, demand, and unfair" are terms that—when used often—indicate a potential sinkhole eroding under the surface of your life.

Listen to yourself! Read what you write! What does your language show—a gratitude for *hesed* or a graceless, disconnected heart?

SO WHAT NOW?

1. Stop right now and thank God for calling you. Write a thank you note to the Lord, describing how wonderful it is to be one of the "called children of God."

2. If you were to develop a memory tool for gratitude, what would work well for you? Prayerfully consider starting that practice today.

3. Think through your communication over the past week. What does an honest appraisal of your language display about your gratitude or lack thereof?

CHAPTER 4

FOSTERING GRATITUDE

> THEME: God calls us to a lifestyle choice of encouraging others. This is a beautiful picture of Christ-empowered living, where His people spur others on toward an attitude of gratitude. This only happens when we begin with hearts grateful for God's love toward us.
>
> OBJECTIVE: That we gratefully spur our brethren to love.

The Glory of Their Times is a baseball book. It was produced in 1966 and details the lives of ballplayers from the early modern era. It is, quite frankly, the finest baseball book ever written. Further, it is one of the best collections of oral history ever produced. Larry Richards arranges the material so well, that expert critics have this to say about it:

> Ted Williams: It has been a long time since I enjoyed a book as much as I enjoyed *The Glory of Their Times*…The day after I finished it, I started reading it again.
>
> Stephen Jay Gould in *The New York Times Book Review:* I could happily reread every summer for the rest of my life this greatest of all baseball books.[36]

I mention this because of how that book is connected to this book you are currently reading. A portion of this chapter comes from a speech I gave at a conference many years ago. At that gathering, I taught on the connection between gratitude and love. After I spoke, an anonymous package came for me in the mail. In the package was *The Glory of Their Times* along with a note that read:

> I don't know if you like baseball, but even if you don't you should read this book. It came out 25 years ago and is the best baseball book ever written. I am sending the book as a thank you for your discussion of gratitude and encouragement. I think that talk will prove to be like this book. 25 years from now that Bible study will still be the most important thing Christians need to hear.[37]

How encouraging! As I was pulling this study on gratitude together I remembered that note, noticing that some of that old talk really does fit well here. So even though I don't know who gave me the great note and greater book, I hope he ends up with a copy of this book somehow and smiles.

LOVE ONE ANOTHER.

The critical issue in the discussion the man referenced is Christ's command in 2 John:

> Now I ask you, lady, not as though *I were* writing to you a new commandment, but the one which we have had from the beginning, that we love one another. And this is love, that we walk according to His commandments. This is the commandment, just as you have heard from the beginning, that you should walk in it. (2 John 5-6 NASB)

The point is pretty clear, is it not? God commands Christians to love one another. That is the calling. The Apostle John is addressing a "lady and her children" in this letter. Most biblical scholars think this is a euphemism for a local church and its members. It could be just one family who all trust Jesus, and the meaning would be basically unchanged; but the more likely scenario is that the aged John is addressing a church.[38]

God, through His apostle, addresses this church and reminds them of Jesus' primary decree—His followers are meant to love each other. Period. Now, I should let you in on a little pastoral secret. People read this verse—and the passages in John's gospel where Jesus first gave the order—and it makes Christians all zealous about doing nice things for each other. That's why pastors like to teach these texts so often. People get all loving when reminded that we are to be known by our love. And that's great...

But there's a problem. It doesn't *last.* The initial push of affection runs out. As you know, loving people is hard work! Humans are stinky. We are demanding and irritable and frankly rather stupid. It's really tiring to love such creatures. Pets are much easier to love.

Still, the committed Christian hears John telling him to love the brethren. So, he bucks up, sets his jaw, and works very hard to love other humans just as difficult to love as he is himself. Often the Christian will go looking for a new shot of what one of our pastors calls "love adrenaline"—a sort of brotherly affection steroid shot found in a book, a conference, a concert, etc. And those can be great, but love adrenaline doesn't last either. Rarely does it make it through the parking lot—where all those "brethren" we're committed to love become "idiots" that we wish God would take out of our way.

The point is that just trying to love people in our strength is impossible. We have to do this love thing God's way, by *His* power. You see, our love for people is only possible because of the love of God.

GROUNDED IN THE LOVE OF GOD

Look at the very beginning of the letter of 2 John: "The elder to the chosen lady and her children, whom I love in truth" (2 John 1 NASB) "Chosen" is a really important idea. *Eklektos* [ek leck tose'] means selected for a purpose. It's quite similar to the Hebrew term *bahir* [bay here]– a word the Hebrews used for someone set aside by the God of Israel for His pleasure and plan.

God chooses His church, something also expounded in Paul's writings. God chooses His people for His pleasure and His plan. And here we discover that God's choosing becomes the foundation from which true love flows. As John wrote in a different letter: "We love, because He first loved us." (1 John 4:19 NASB)

Here's a great summary of "chosen" in 2 John 1 from theologian D. L. Akin:

She is "chosen" because God elected her to belong to himself. God called the lady and those who comprise her family to be his own. The fact that she is chosen ["by God" is clearly implied] indicates the initiative of her election was with God and that her privileged position is not accidental. The spiritual status believers enjoy is the result of God's grace and goodness.[39]

In other words, all love for people is forged in *gratitude*. We can only love and *keep on loving* because God loves us. He empowers us to love by choosing to love us first. This is what Christians so often miss. It's why we wear out and stop loving as soon as things get rough. We neglect to live by the 2 John "choosing," forgetting that all love is grounded in gratitude.

I must first be grateful to God for what He's done. Then I can do what God wants done. I must be grateful for His love for me (verse 1), then I can love others (verse 5). The classical Roman Senator Cicero seemed to grasp this idea. That pagan was a talented thinker and he stumbled unto this reality, writing, "Gratitude is not only the greatest of virtues, but also the parent of all others."[40]

WALK IN THIS.

John reminds us to love our brethren in Christ. This can be done because we are grateful for God's choosing. And it's not optional. In John's memorable phraseology, we are to "walk in this." Walk is a handy phrase for all of living. In classical use "walk" describes how one lives every day, all day. We still use a form of this today. We describe careers as "walks of life."

Every week at church I see children who are learning to walk. It's a beautiful, bumpy adventure. And it's fascinating what that transition into walking does in the parent. As a crawler becomes a toddler, the parent usually starts thinking more about all of that child's life to come. There is something about walking that strikes a chord in us. It makes us consider how one's days are spent.

For example, when musician John Fischer's son Christopher was just starting to consider walking, John wrote this beautiful poem:

> Christopher knows Christopher's toes
> He just found them today
> Stuck in the air at the end of his chair
> Ten little toes just waiting to play
> It's hard to believe that these little feet
> Will walk into the next generation
> May they be feet that bring the gospel of peace
> To every situation[41]

A father prays that his child will walk…live…according to the good news of God's love. That's what John desires as well. John shows a commitment to three things in the letters we call 2 and 3 John: love; truth; and walk, i.e., the practical living of love and truth. And it all starts with gratitude. It all begins with a remembrance of God's gracious choosing.

THE WAY OF DIOTREPHES

Sadly, when gratitude is missing, there is no walk in love. John describes this horrible scenario in the next book over in 3 John: 8-11.

> Therefore we ought to support people like these, that we may be fellow workers for the truth. I have written something to the church, but Diotrephes, who likes to put himself first, does not acknowledge our authority. So if I come, I will bring up what he is doing, talking wicked nonsense against us. And not content with that, he refuses to welcome the brothers, and also stops those who want to and puts them out of the church. Beloved, do not imitate evil but imitate good. Whoever does good is from God; whoever does evil has not seen God. (3 John 8-11 ESV)

In our notes, we call this the way of Diotrephes [Dee oh tref' ess]. Diotrephes is a stinker, is he not? By the way, I don't know if that's his real name or a nickname John gave the guy. You see, Diotrephes means "cherished of Zeus" or "increase of Zeus." This could be a given name of a Greek man who came to trust in Jesus. Most people kept their pagan given names even after becoming Christians.

But, this is a somewhat unique name and it could be that John calls this dude "cherished of Zeus" as a way to make clear that the guy is working against the one true God. I had a seminary prof who used to describe theologians who denied Jesus' deity as "members of Hell's Hall of Fame." That's kind of like saying "Diotrephes."

So what comprises the way of Diotrephes? Firstly, *we see people through jealous eyes*. Verse 8 is describing God's expectations of hospitality in the early churches. Most churches in the first two centuries did not have set pastors. Only in large cities—and that only rarely—did a church have an Elder gifted in teaching the scriptures.

Some writers said that having such a pastor retained in your own church fellowship all year was like having a lampstand that gave light all day and night. You were part of a really blessed church if you had your own lamp all the time to illuminate God's Word.

But such dedicated, site-specific preachers were rare. Instead, most churches made use of travelling teachers. These guys were continuing an old Hebraic and Greco-Roman tradition with a twist. The ancient rabbis and philosophers would travel around with their students in tow, teaching through life and travel. These new pastors also travelled—but *to* their students instead of with them. The people would gather on Sundays (some still apparently on Saturdays) and study the Bible with the preacher.

The preachers didn't go to seminary, as there weren't any, but they were gifted by God and they did study hard. They carried letters of approval from apostles or church leaders in Christian centers like Jerusalem, Antioch, or Gamla. Letters flew back and forth along the Roman post system, setting the preacher's travel schedules. The sheer volume of their correspondence astonishes people today. Those people wrote letters at about the same clip that we send texts.

Those letters often concerned the travelling teacher's needs. The guy would arrive in town on say Thursday and need food, lodging, a quiet space to study until church met Sunday night. Then he'd need a little money to get on to the next town in his circuit.

Diotrephes has no appreciation for this. He refuses to engage in supporting and submitting to these approved teachers. He does not give thanks for God's grace in sending their church the light of scripture taught by a gifted preacher! No. Diotrephes is selfish and does not extend love graciously to this other leader. In fact, Diotrephes won't even allow other people in the church to take in the traveling Bible teachers. Wow. What selfishness! Aren't you grateful that no one is like that today!

I have many friends that are missionaries in remote, dark, and difficult places in the world. Their lifestyle is a little different from the 1st century traveling preacher, but there are parallels. When those missionaries are back in Texas with us, what do they need? They need a place to stay and the use of a car. They often need some spending money because it's usually more expensive to live and eat here. They need to be introduced to new people who might be moved of God to help further their mission. They could use a quiet getaway where they can rest and study.

And yet, you'd be surprised how rarely missionaries receive those things. I trust you would be horrified at what I've seen: pastors who are jealous of the missionaries' attention; people who invite the missionaries to lunch and stick the poor missionaries with the bill; people with extra cars sitting in the driveway who just close their eyes to the bulletin note that a missionary needs transport for a few days. It is astonishing how often people tend toward the Diotrephan way, which is the opposite of what God wants for us.

Go back to verse 9. We discover what's really driving Diotrephes and all of us when we see through jealous eyes: "I wrote unto the church: but Diotrephes, who loveth to have the preeminence among them, receiveth us not." (3 John 9 KJV)

"Preeminence" is *philoproteuo* [feel oh pro tee' you oh]. It means the love of being first; the need to be seen as #1. You may be the smartest, most talented person on earth, but when you are driven by a rabid love of being first you will not love your brethren. In fact, you will come off like a petty jerk.

Notice the grasping, driven, insecure attitude in Diotrephes. This is not a grateful person. This is a man pushing himself forward because he lacks the confidence of God's choosing. He cannot abide the thought that someone else has talent or authority. He even rejects God's Word—or at least the parts that he doesn't like. This is the jealous leveling spirit—a desire to pull everyone else down to his miserable, dank basement.

The other part of Diotrephes' way is to *demand ungodly uniformity*. Look again at verses 10-11: "For this reason, if I come, I will call attention to his deeds which he does, unjustly accusing us with wicked words; and not satisfied with this, he himself does not receive the brethren, either, and he forbids those who desire *to do so* and puts *them* out of the church. Beloved, do not imitate what is evil, but what is good. The one who does good is of God; the one who does evil has not seen God."

Diotrephes ignores God's words and demands everybody line up with his own ideas. We already saw that the guy rejects aspects of scripture—from God's apostle! He throws out the parts that he doesn't like. Then he slaps ugly labels on anyone who disagrees. Wow! Can you imagine that kind of hubris! Thank goodness that never occurs in our day…

As a child in Oklahoma, I remember the collapse of the rust belt economies and the flood of immigrants from Michigan. Mostly I remember the wildly popular bumper stickers around our town that read "Yankee go home." Not exactly a spirit of hospitality. A similar attitude was exposed in 2014 when Governor Cuomo of New York gave an astonishing speech in which he declared, "Republicans are not welcome in New York." And anyone today who dares disagree with the current homosexual social agenda is excoriated as "homophobic" and forced into rethink concentration camps known by the Orwellian title of "sensitivity training." People today are experts on ungodly uniformity. And that's just in America! We lack space to describe Communist, Arab, and some European societies. They're worse!

These uniformities are not based on Scripture. In fact, they are decidedly unscriptural. Just like Diotrephes, our current uniformists throw out all parts of scripture they don't like. It's not just other people who do this. I can do this! I easily slip into rewriting Jesus into my own image. I take a little of the four real gospels, throw in a healthy dash of my own ideas, and voila! I live by the Gospel according to Wayne. And then, as a church leader, I could demand a bunch of people live by my bastardized truth.

Shudder. Isn't Diotrephes' way horrible! No gratitude in Christ and thus no walk in love with other Christians.

THE WAY OF GAIUS

So, let's leave that mess behind and learn the opposite. When gratitude is present, there is a beautiful walk in love. This is exactly what we learn from a wonderful person named Gaius. Read 3 John 1-8:

> The elder to the beloved Gaius, whom I love in truth. Beloved, I pray that all may go well with you and that you may be in good health, as it goes well with your soul. For I rejoiced greatly when the brothers came and testified to your truth, as indeed you are walking in the truth. I have no greater joy than to hear that my children are walking in the truth. Beloved, it is a faithful thing you do in all your efforts for these brothers, strangers as they are, who testified to your love before the church. You will do well to send them on their journey in a manner worthy of God. For they have gone out for the sake of the name, accepting nothing from the Gentiles. Therefore we ought to support people like these, that we may be fellow workers for the truth. (3 John 1-8 ESV)

Gaius [guy' yos] is probably not a nickname, but it's a cool name nonetheless. It means "of the land" and describes somebody dependable and solid. The way of dependable Gaius is to *actively love your brothers,* even the ones you don't know.

My wife, Janna, and I showed up in an extremely remote village high in the mountains of Guatemala. A friend of ours was translating the Bible into the native tongue, and had invited us to bring a crash of 30 high school and college students to help build houses for villagers made homeless by Marxist terrorists who had burned the homes of those who wouldn't join their rebellion.

But when we arrived, the missionary friend was gone. Gone! He had an emergency that took him down to Cuidad, Guatemala. The church people had no idea why we were there. The non-Christians in town assumed we were yet more Marxist murderers and frankly wanted to run us off the mountain or worse. But the lead Elder in the church took charge. In broken Spanish we communicated. And he declared we were brethren. Further, he led the whole church and village to welcome us. They even gave what little food they had to feed our ravenous students.

Of course, once we started building houses for these poor widows and orphans, then everything changed. And once I started teaching the Bible at night, much of the village gathered to study with us. But here's what stuck with me—they actively loved us as brothers in Christ even <u>before</u> they knew we were going to be useful to them. That is the way of Gaius.

God is calling for that kind of brotherly love—for active love. Look at the transitive, action verbals that describe Gaius' leadership in our text:

> ³ you *are walking* in truth. I have no greater joy than this, to hear of my children *walking* in the truth. Beloved, you *are acting* faithfully in whatever you *accomplish* for the brethren, and especially *when they are* strangers; and they have testified to your love before the church. You will *do well* to *send* them on their way in a manner worthy of God. (3 John 3-6 NASB, emphases added)

I received a great note from my pulpit team partner Randall Satchell about this:

> We need to stop *sitting* in Christ's commandments and do more *walking* in them. It's good to feel grateful, but it's also good to spread some grateful. Like "Kid President" so aptly said in 2015, "Your heart's beating, you got breath coming through your nose—it's time to DO something!"

Speaking of the pulpit team, look at this wonderful letter I received recently from a new person at our church:

> Wayne, for the entire first year I attended Frisco Bible, I had an incredible fascination with a mysterious and elusive ministry hiding in the shadows—the FBC *puppet* team. Who

were these people? Why do they have so much wisdom? Why do they get to preview your sermons ahead of time? And yet…I still haven't seen them put on a single puppet show?! Imagine the look on my face one Sunday when I realized it was the *pulpit* team![42]

Gaius' way is to actively love the brethren—whether they are on the pulpit team or the puppet team. Gaius's way also involves *showing gratitude*. This is what the traveling teachers did. See how they stood and testified about Gaius? They told other people about this wonderful church leadership that loved God's family.

And, as we've already seen, gratitude is the basis of Gaius' love. That's what Gaius and the church do when taking in the teachers—they are showing gratitude for the privilege of being a part of the great ministry to God. Look in the passage! This is also what John is doing. He is applauding with a grateful heart. He is grateful and full of joy he writes in verse 4. John is expressing his gratitude for people obeying Jesus' commands.

This is why thank you notes are so powerful. Same is true for public testimonies or even tweets praising God for someone. It's a big, sustaining circle of gratefulness and hope. Showing appreciation engenders the gratitude that we know changes everything. This perpetuates the cycle and drives people to seek the Lord.

There's an online business leadership community called "Unstuck." Recently, I was alerted to this post on their site:

> When put into practice, gratitude creates a virtuous circle. It fosters contentment, joy, respect, and connection to our world and the people in it. Gratitude makes us feel good inside. And when we share it, other people feel good inside. And you know what happens then: The feel-good-insiders send their goodwill to more people, who in turn start feeling good inside. Good feelings boomerang everywhere.[43]

It's delightful to watch this happen. Here's a scenario I have observed many, many times. The non-Christian is lonely out in a world run by Diotrephes. But by God's grace, she bumps into one of you, a Christian who has committed, loving relationships based in gratitude. Intrigued, she accepts your invitation to come to a Bible study or small group meeting or church service.

There, she wrestles with the thing she's spent years trying to avoid—the real Person of Jesus. She recognizes that all your love comes from gratefulness to Jesus. Then she has to finally face the facts and consider whether Jesus is a lunatic...a liar...or the Lord He claimed to be. Usually, she trusts in Jesus as Savior. And suddenly, she becomes the thankful one, shining forth the way of Gaius for the next person to come along. It's beautiful.

Let's review this simple but profound contrast. In a nutshell, here is John's gratitude thesis in the two letters:

- I can violate Jesus' love command by being jealous and demanding uniformity like the capitol in *The Hunger Games*.

- Or I can actively love, showing thanks like Gaius.

PAUL'S CONTRIBUTION TO GAIUS' WAY

For full understanding, we should bring in another voice on this issue. The apostle Paul also taught about fulfilling Jesus' love calling. Let's consider the Apostle Paul's contribution to thankful, active loving. Paul provides four powerful ideas. First, *Acknowledge and praise the source of your love.* That's what we learn in 1 Timothy 1:

> But I received mercy for this reason, that in me, as the foremost [sinner], Jesus Christ might display his perfect patience as an example to those who were to believe in him for eternal life. To the King of the ages, immortal, invisible, the only God, be honor and glory forever and ever. Amen. (1 Timothy 1:16-17 ESV)

Paul is not blowing smoke. He realizes just how ugly his natural soul is. And he recognizes the amazing grace of God that has saved Him through Jesus' substitutionary death and resurrection. That releases a paean of praise that just can't be held back! Paul acknowledges and praises God who is the source of all love.

Is that true of us? Do we remember just how rich is the love shown to us by the Lord? Do we keep in mind how incredibly wonderful it is that God chooses to love goof balls like us? If not, our active love will quickly lose its gratitude base and devolve into mere politeness.

Paul's second concept is to ***accept scripturally-legitimate points of view***. Look at Romans 14:

> One person believes he may eat anything, while the weak person eats only vegetables. Let not the one who eats despise the one who abstains, and let not the one who abstains pass judgment on the one who eats, for God has welcomed him. Who are you to pass judgment on the servant of another? It is before his own master that he stands or falls. And he will be upheld, for the Lord is able to make him stand. (Romans 14:2-4 ESV)

Is it scripturally acceptable for a New Testament Christian to keep kosher a kitchen? Yes! Of course. No, they can't confuse that with a way to earn God's favor. Legalism is forbidden. But if you praise God best by excluding bacon, more power to you.

At the same time, is it OK for a Jesus-believer to feast on bacon and catfish? Yes indeed! That is patently clear in the Bible. God tells the very Jewish Peter to declare nothing unholy. The Hebrew of Hebrews Paul later reminds Peter of the lesson. The point is that—in food as in all else—perspectives that do not violate the wide boundaries of scripture are all to be accepted. This is the opposite of Diotrephes' extra-biblical dogmatism.

Nonetheless, last week I saw two postings by wonderful young Christians whom I love:

- The first said, "If you eat Gluten you are an idiot. Read this study and repent."
- The second post read, "If you went to Hogwarts and said you won't eat Gluten, you would be immediately consigned to Hufflepuff."

I think Paul and Gaius would appreciate each perspective…and probably rebuke them both. I also know that Paul would pray for them, as I did. He wrote: "I thank God whom I serve, as did my ancestors, with a clear conscience, as I remember you constantly in my prayers night and day." 2 Timothy 1:3 ESV)

Herein lies Paul's third contribution to Gaius' way—*pray for the brethren.* That's the most actively loving thing anyone can do. And notice that Paul's loving prayers are founded in his thanks to God. When one is grateful, one is drawn to pray for others to be blessed as well.

Our church staff and Elders take considerable time every week to pray through a whole bunch of prayer cards we receive every week. Why would we do that when there is so much work to do? Because this is how one loves. We thank God for our brethren and we then remember them in prayer before the God who calls and loves each of us.

Fourth, Paul shows Christians to *spur others to love and courage.* A sentence later, 2 Timothy 1 adds: "For this reason I remind you to fan into flame the gift of God, which is in you through the laying on of my hands, for God gave us a spirit not of fear but of power and love and self-control." (2 Timothy 1:6-7 ESV)

Loving people doesn't mean letting them vegetate. A true friend spurs you on! Real love coaches me, cheers me on, and won't let me grow complacent. Real active love says: "Fan the flame! Quit being fearful! Get to work by God's power. Be disciplined!"

Think! Real love encourages the other person. That's the meaning of the word! En-courage = to put courage inside another. Hebrews 10:24 has a memorable rendering of the idea: "Let us consider how to stimulate one another to love and good deeds." (Hebrews 10:24 NASB)

The Glory of Their Times—that greatest oral history—has this fabulous story from Hall of Famer and Washington Senators star, Goose Goslin:

> One year I was hitting way out in front of everybody else in the league by 20 or 30 points all season. That was 1928. But in September Heinie Manush kept gaining and gaining and gaining on me, and by the last day of the season he was only a fraction of a point behind me. We played the St. Louis

Browns on the last day, and Heinie played left field for the Browns. I was in left field for the Senators. So Heinie and I were playing against each other, with the batting title on the line.

Well, do you know that battle went right down to my very last time at bat. It came to my turn at bat in the ninth inning of the last game of the season, and if I make an out I lose the batting championship, and if I get a hit I win it – his average is .378 and mine is .378 and a fraction. If I get up and don't get a hit, I'll drop below him. I had that information before I went to bat. One of the sportswriters sent it down to me, with a note that said: "If you go to bat and make an out, Manush will win the batting title. Best thing to do is don't get up to bat at all, and then you've got it made."

Gee, I didn't know what to do. [Manager] Bucky Harris left it up to me…"What do you want to do, Goose?" he asked me. "It's up to you. I'll send in a pinch hitter if you want me to."

"Well, I've never won a batting title and I sure would love to, just for once in my life. So I think I'll stay right here on the bench, if it's OK with you."

Of course, everybody gathered around, wanting to be in on what's going on. "You better watch out," Joe Judge says, "or they'll call you yellow."

"What are you talking about?"

"Well," he says, "There's Manush right there in left field. What do you think he'll figure if you win the title by sitting on the bench?"

So this starts a big argument in the dugout: should I go up or shouldn't I? Finally, I got disgusted with the whole thing. "All right, all right," I said, "Stop all this noise. I'm going up there."

And doggone if that pitcher didn't get two quick strikes on me before I could even get set in the batter's box. I never took my bat off my shoulder, and already the count was 2 strikes and no balls. So I turned around and stepped out of the box and sort of had a discussion with myself, while I put some dirt on my hands…

Well, I didn't know what to do. And then it came to me—get thrown out of the ballgame! That way, I wouldn't be charged with a time at bat, and it was in the bag. The umpire was a big-necked guy by the name of Bill Guthrie, so I turned on him.

"Why, those pitches weren't even close," I said.

"Listen, wise guy," he says, "There's no such thing as close or not close. It's either *dis* or *dat*."

Oh, did that ever get me mad (I acted like). I called him every name in the book, I stepped on his toes, I pushed him, I did everything.

"OK," he said, after about five minutes of this, "are you ready to bat now? You're not going to get thrown out of this ball game no matter *what* you do, so you might as well get up to that plate. If I wanted to throw you out, I'd throw you clear over to Oshkosh. But you're going to bat, and you better be in there *swinging*, too. No bases on balls, you hear me?"

I heard him. And gee, you know—I got a lucky hit. Saved me. I guess that hit was the biggest thrill I ever got.[44]

We need to spur our teammates on the same way. Goose's teammates, the umpire, everybody spurred Goose to do the disciplined and courageous thing. That's what the way of Gaius does! It's what John and Paul do writing these letters. These notes love and encourage the brethren.

SO WHAT NOW?

It's our turn! Let's not end this chapter without acting on truth.

1. Take a few seconds and write a note right now! Encourage someone. Spur them to love and good deeds. Apologize. Sow appreciation or acceptance. You can mail or deliver them later, but let's write them now—no base on balls. Step up to the plate and thank someone.

2. Personalize what we've learned. List below three people in your life who could and should learn the power of gratitude just by interacting with you.

3. In a serious time of prayer, confess the Diotrephes aspects of your living. Ask God to guide you from that to the way of Gaius.

CONCLUSION

Remember A. A. Milne's description of Piglet? "Piglet noticed that even though he had a very small heart, it could hold a rather large amount of gratitude."⁴⁵ A. A. Milne, understanding the life-changing power of gratitude, describes something applicable to us all. Every single heart can hold an incredibly large amount of gratitude.

There is amazing power in a merry heart. When I develop my aptitude for gratitude, the results are astonishing—in my life and in the lives of those around me. And the only foundation that genuinely establishes lasting gratefulness in the unending love of God. That's why Psalm 100 declares:

> Shout joyfully to the LORD, all the earth.
> Serve the LORD with gladness;
> Come before Him with joyful singing.
> Know that the LORD Himself is God;
> It is He who has made us, and not we ourselves;
> *We are* His people and the sheep of His pasture.
>
> Enter His gates with thanksgiving
> *And* His courts with praise.
> Give thanks to Him, bless His name.
> For the LORD is good;
> His lovingkindness is everlasting
> And His faithfulness to all generations. (Psalm 100 NASB)

Why is there joyful shouting and glad serving? Because YHWH is God. Why can we enter His presence with thanksgiving and praise? Because He has made us His people through the grace of the Messiah. Why do we give thanks and bless God? Because His *hesed* never ends.

Our merry hearts are instituted and maintained on the foundation of God's grace.

These short chapters and exercises are designed to help build such joyful hearts in each of us. If you find the book helpful, please pass it on. If you develop other practices that help foster thankfulness, please pass those on as well—to others and to me. I would be delighted to hear from you! I can be reached through allthedifference@friscobible.com.

ACKNOWLEDGEMENTS

Hilariously, we were far along in this book process before I noticed that the acknowledgements had been left out. How ironic would it prove to write a book on gratitude that doesn't contain thanks! Happily, we caught the mistake and I can take a moment to express appreciation for those who have made this possible.

Dr. Tim Demy piloted the project brilliantly. Amy Cole of JPL did excellent work on design and layout. The Frisco Bible Church pulpit team was deeply involved in shaping the ideas in this book, just as they continue to shape me. Thanks to David Wade, Tracy Bush, Fran Legband, Cindy Sharp, Randall Satchell, and Martin MacDonald. Carolyn Powell once again served as the eagle-eyed proofreader. The *All The Difference* team continues to ensure that we are able to share God's Word in ways that make all the difference in people's lives. Well done and thank you, Bush, Hahn, Havens, Siems, Hooper, Sipes, Portillo, and Miller families. Finally, our family – Janna, Jessica, Grant, Mike, and Ben – once again supported and encouraged throughout. They truly make hearts merry.

ENDNOTES

1. John Milton, *Paradise Lost*, (London: Penguin, 2012 reprint of 1667 ed.), Book IV, l. 55.

2. Mark Twain, *Pudd'nhead Wilson's Calendar* (New York: Harcourt, 1974 reprint of 1894. edition), 11.

3. David Horsager, *The Trust Edge*, (New York: Free Press/Simon and Schuster, 2009), 39.

4. Diana Kapp, *Wall Street Journal*, 23 December, 2013; page 7.

5. Ibid.

6. Mark Altrogge, "Forever Grateful" on *Romans*, (Nashville: Benson, 1989).

7. Billy Crockett, "Thankful Boys and Girls" on *Red Bird Blue Sky*, (Nashville: Sparrow, 1995).

8. For a statistical analysis of similar surveys, see Adler, M. G., & Fagley, N. S. (2005). "Appreciation: Individual Differences in Finding Value and Meaning as a Unique Predictor of Subjective Well-Being." *Journal of Personality*, 73 (1), 79-114.

9. *Wall Street Journal*, 23 December, 2013; page 8.

10. R. E. Averbeck, *NIDOTTE* 2:689.

11. Phil Vischer, "The Thankfulness Song" in *Madame Blueberry*, (Nashville: Big Idea!, 2005).

12. Todd Sinelli, Todd, *True Riches*, (Dallas: Lit Torch, 2013), 46.

13 Paul Hahn, private correspondence, in author's collection, used with permission.

14 David Horsager, *The Trust Edge*, (New York: Free Press/Simon and Schuster, 2009), 39.

15 Private correspondence, in author's collection.

16 Randy Glasbergen, "Attitude of Gratitude" cartoon, MH 27. United Features, 2004. Used with permission.

17 Twenge and Kasser, "Generational Changes in Materialism and Work Centrality, 1976-2007" *Personality and Social Psychology Bulletin*, vol. 39, 7: pp. 883-897. First published May 1, 2013. [Note: you might also enjoy Dr. Twenge's book, *Generation Me*.]

18 Private correspondence, in author's collection.

19 David Wade, personal correspondence in author's collection. The pulpit team are lay persons who help me think through upcoming teaching series and evaluate every message I give. They have been an incredible blessing in my development, and I would be honored to help you establish a team in your church. Just write allthedifference@friscobible.com.

20 Personal correspondence, in author's collection.

21 Personal correspondence, in author's collection.

22 Justin Martyr, *Apologia* [*First Apology*] from the Internet, 23 June 2017.

23 B. Bannister and M. V. Hudson, "Praise the Lord," New York: Warner, 1979.

24 Image courtesy Florida Geological Survey.

25 Gordon MacDonald, *Ordering Your Private World*, (Atlanta: Oliver Nelson, 1985), 36-37.

26 If you want to learn more about the Puritan's reliance upon God, I recommend Arthur Bennett's collection of Puritan prayers titled *The Valley of Vision*.

27 Stanley E. Jones, E. Stanley, *The Divine Yes*, (Nashville: Abingdon, 1991), 63.

28 John Quincy Adams, *Letters of John Quincy Adams, to his son, on the Bible and its teachings* (Auburn, N.Y.: Derby Miller, 1848) 112.

29 Michael Braudrick, "Gift of Grace," 2016.

30 See Matthew 18.

31 Michael Braudrick, "Through the Eyes of a Child," 2016.

32 Please grasp what that is saying. Give as a lifestyle and you are less likely to experience the sinkhole syndrome when it rains.

33 Arthur C. Brooks, "Giving is Good For You" *Wall Street Journal*, November 25, 2013, page 9.

34 Beth Greenfield, "Gratitude Changed Her" *Yahoo Style*, March 2, 2014.

35 Lynne, Scrivens, *Facebook* post, December 31, 2013.

36 Quotes courtesy Quill Press, 1984.

37 Private correspondence, in author's collection. Note: for the record, the Braudricks absolutely love baseball.

38 Verse 13 especially indicates a church and not one family, as it seems unlikely that John would know more about a lady's extended family than the lady would herself. He would, however, know more about a sister church.

39 D. L. Akin, *1,2,3 John*, (Nashville: Broadman and Holman, 2001), 49.

40 Marcus Tullius Cicero, *Pro Plancio*, in *Cicero* (Cambridge: Harvard/Loeb, 1923), 406.

41 John Fischer, "Christopher's Toes," Waco: Interlinc, 1987.

42 Private correspondence, in author's collection.

43 "Unstuck," online post *November 25, 2013.*

44 Lawrence Richards, *The Glory of Their Times* (New York: Quill, 1966), 282-83.

45 Milne, A.A., *Winnie the Pooh* (New York: Puffin, 1992), 49.

ABOUT THE AUTHOR

Wayne Braudrick serves as Senior Pastor of Frisco Bible Church in Frisco, Texas. He also teaches through the *All the Difference* daily radio broadcast and serves as adjunct faculty for Ouachita Baptist University. Dr. Braudrick earned his doctorate in leadership communication through Middlesex University in London; gained a master's degree in Bible at Dallas Theological Seminary; and was a National Merit Scholar at Baylor University where he read history, literature, and education. Wayne lives with his marvelous family in Frisco, Texas, where he and his wife refuse to let work come in the way of their regular racquetball games.

OTHER BOOKS BY WAYNE BRAUDRICK:

WHATEVER HAPPENED TO MANHOOD—
BOOK AND COMPANION STUDY GUIDE

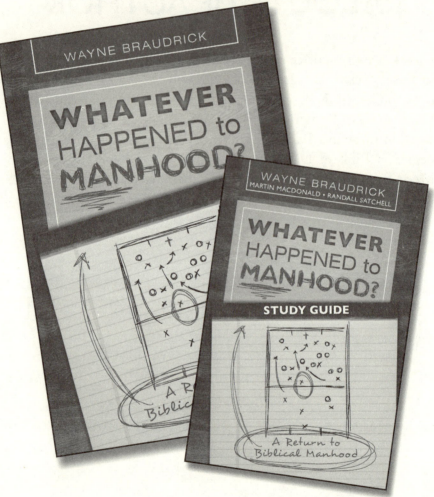

LOOK FOR THIS BOOK AND OTHER
GREAT TITLES AT: LAMPIONPRESS.COM

ALSO AVAILABLE:
FOR SUCH A TIME AS THIS... BIBLICAL WOMEN CHANGING THE WORLD

LOOK FOR THIS BOOK AND OTHER GREAT TITLES AT: LAMPIONPRESS.COM

All the Difference exists to engage you with the **Bible** in a way that makes all the difference in your life.

atd ALL THE DIFFERENCE™

THE RADIO TEACHING MINISTRY OF DR. WAYNE BRAUDRICK

allthedifference.us

Broadcast schedule • Listen online • Sign up for weekly email